JOURNALISM AND TRUTH

Medill School of Journalism
VISIONS *of the* AMERICAN PRESS

GENERAL EDITOR
David Abrahamson

Other titles in this series

HERBERT J. GANS
Deciding What's News: A Study of CBS Evening News, NBC Nightly
News, Newsweek, *and* Time

MAURINE H. BEASLEY
First Ladies and the Press: The Unfinished Partnership of the Media Age

PATRICIA BRADLEY
Women and the Press: The Struggle for Equality

DAVID A. COPELAND
The Idea of a Free Press: The Enlightenment and Its Unruly Legacy

MICHAEL SWEENEY
The Military and the Press: An Uneasy Truce

PATRICK S. WASHBURN
The African American Newspaper: Voice of Freedom

DAVID R. SPENCER
The Yellow Journalism: The Press and America's Emergence as World Power

KARLA GOWER
Public Relations and the Press: The Troubled Embrace

JOURNALISM
AND TRUTH
STRANGE BEDFELLOWS

Tom Goldstein

Foreword by Howard H. Baker, Jr.

MEDILL SCHOOL OF JOURNALISM

Northwestern University Press
Evanston, Illinois

Northwestern University Press
www.nupress.northwestern.edu

Copyright © 2007 by Tom Goldstein
Published 2007 by Northwestern University Press.
All rights reserved.

Printed in the United States of America

10 9 8 7 6 5 4 3 2 1

ISBN 978-0-8101-2433-2

Library of Congress Cataloging-in-Publication Data

Goldstein, Tom.
  Journalism and truth : strange bedfellows / Tom Goldstein ;
foreword by Howard H. Baker, Jr.
      p. cm. — (Visions of the American press)
  Includes bibliographical references and index.
  ISBN-13: 978-0-8101-2433-2 (pbk. : alk. paper)
  ISBN-10: 0-8101-2433-5 (pbk. : alk. paper)
  1. Journalism—United States. 2. Truth. 3.
Journalism—Objectivity—United States. I. Title. II. Series.
PN4888.O25G65 2007
071.3—dc22

2007007862

∞ The paper used in this publication meets the minimum
requirements of the American National Standard for Information
Sciences—Permanence of Paper for Printed Library Materials,
ANSI Z39.48-1992.

For Leslie, Max, and Blaze

CONTENTS

◈

FOREWORD

◈

Howard H. Baker, Jr.

The search for truth, as Tom Goldstein so ably demonstrates, is a much more ambitious and profound pursuit than the mere accumulation of facts, even when assembled with the most stringent adherence to accuracy. Journalists, who produce what the late *Washington Post* publisher Philip Graham called "the first rough draft of history," know better than anyone that their daily reporting is incomplete, that the truth of a matter emerges more slowly than a newspaper deadline demands, that it is best to avoid the pretense of omniscience when so much remains obscured from view. National leaders, too, know that the intelligence they receive from the agencies responsible for gathering and analyzing information on which momentous decisions rest is almost always incomplete and imperfect. But the leaders' decisions, like the journalists' deadlines, often cannot wait for the last question to be asked and answered, for the final salient fact to be ascertained.

Historians looking through the rearview mirror at events often convey a sense of inevitability about them, but decision makers and journalists do not have that luxury. We see, as Saint Paul said, "through a glass, darkly," and do the best we can with the fragmentary knowledge available at the moment of decision or deadline. Because politicians and journalists share this perspective, this frustration with the fragmentary, it has always been a mystery to me why the two sides have so little apparent sympathy for the limitations on one another's grasp of a given situation. To be sure, some political leaders have been known to have their minds made up on a course of action, with facts to the contrary being viewed as "inconvenient truths." And journalists are routinely criticized for bringing a bias to their coverage that only accommodates facts that fit their fixed point of view.

But in my experience, most politicians and journalists want to get it right, to follow wherever the facts may lead, to draw conclusions based on the best information available. But this approach is not without risk. When as vice chairman of the Senate Watergate Committee I announced that I would go where the facts led me, I was denounced by many of my fellow Republicans for not mounting a more vigorous (and blinkered) defense of President Nixon. Nor did I endear myself to my party when, a few years later, I decided to retain consultants on both sides of the Panama Canal treaty issue and commission them to make the best cases for and against ratification of the treaty to cede American control over the canal to the government of Panama. But I reasoned that the truth of the situation would emerge in this adversarial process—as we have long presumed it to do in our courts of law, where I practiced for years before turning to politics—and I am satisfied that it did.

Truth is not a prisoner of this bipolar process. There may well be more than two sides to an issue, as anyone who has dealt with the old Soviet Union ("a riddle wrapped in enigma inside a mystery," as Churchill described it) or the new Middle East would attest. When as chief of staff for President Reagan I was responsible for the preparation of his decision memoranda, I insisted that only the hardest decisions reach him, the ones for which a good case could be made for several options. In such cases, truth was on many sides of a question, and wisdom and good judgment were required to find our highest national interests in a jungle of competing truths.

Journalists, too, typically have a strong sense of serving the public interest. They consider themselves public servants just as those of us in politics do, and so they should. They ferret out truth when the political impulse may be to conceal it, and they hold the political class accountable to the public between elections. This watchdog role lies at the heart of the First Amendment guaranteeing a free press, and it remains the role the public most wants journalists to play in our society.

The twenty-first century, young as it is, has already produced an entirely new form of journalism—the web log, or "blog"—which actually harkens back to America's colonial days when the lonely pamphleteer could have a significant impact on public debate. As in those earlier days, the modern blogger generally makes no pretense of fairness or scrupulous accuracy, but rather makes a case laden more with opinion than fact, expecting the reader to find "the truth" in the cacophony of contending arguments. This was the modus operandi of American journalism until the last years of the nineteenth century, when my fellow Tennessean Adolph Ochs bought the *New York Times* and promised to present the news "without fear or favor" and with a then-novel fidelity to fact. Other newspapers and magazines, followed later by radio and television, would emulate the *Times's* example for generations.

Today the *Times* itself, like many other prominent newspapers, is often accused of bias, and worse, in its news pages. And the modern consumer of news—particularly the younger consumer—seems willing to accept the notion that a distinct point of view is not a bad thing, that a well-informed opinion may serve the cause of truth more effectively than a dispassionate fact. This may even be right, but the challenge in this modern age of both journalism and politics is to ensure that opinion is, in fact, well informed and tested by reason. Bloggers have no filters as traditional journalists do, no editors to question their assertions and conclusions, and they run the risk of sacrificing credibility in the information marketplace when they detach opinion from fact altogether. Politicians, too, imperil their claim on the public's trust when they advocate policies that appear altogether untethered to reality.

President Reagan was fond of saying that "facts are stubborn things." Former Vice President Gore has made a useful new career of citing "an inconvenient truth" about global warming. Free societies like ours thrive on truth, inconvenient or not, and cannot be free without it. The Bible goes further, arguing that it is the truth itself that makes us free. In all cases, as this thoughtful book by Professor Goldstein so clearly explicates, truth is indispensable. As a self-governing people, we take it lightly, disregard it, or ignore it at our peril.

◈

I spent the summer after my senior year in college working at my hometown newspaper, the *Buffalo Evening News*. It was an idiosyncratic place. On one hand, the paper was suffused in the old newsroom ethos. It was relentless about getting subscribers' names in the paper, whether they had just graduated from elementary school or high school, celebrated a big anniversary—or died. People, or their survivors, would pay to see their names in print, the theory went. On the other hand, the paper was intermittently progressive. For instance, it was one of the first papers to ban cigarette smoking in the newsroom—as a result, there were usually reporters puffing away in the lavatories or on the front sidewalk. I liked the job and thought journalism would be a wonderful way to spend a lifetime. But I was headed for law school at Columbia.

Just before my time was up at the paper, the gruff city editor, Bud Wacker, an ex-marine who was quite the stereotype, asked to meet with me. He had a shaved head and barely spoke to his reporters. Wacker took me aside and told me that instead of going to law school, I should pursue a graduate degree in journalism at Columbia. I was flattered that he spoke to me, but told him it was too late. No, he insisted, I had to reconsider. He arranged an interview with the dean of admissions at Columbia University's Graduate School of Journalism, Chris Trump. First, Trump told me that I was right. It was too late for that year. The class of 1968 had been chosen, and school was about to start. Then we talked. I recited my limited job experience. After my first year in college,

I could not get a salaried job and had signed up selling Fuller Brushes door to door on commission. Surprising my bosses, my parents, and myself, I had done very well knocking on strangers' doors, and, relatively speaking, I made a lot of money doing it. Now I had found a sympathetic ear. Trump had sold Fuller Brushes when he was in college too. (As I later found out, many reporters have had early experiences selling door to door, and for those who, like me, were naturally shy, it was a worthwhile experience.) Trump and I swapped stories about the best strategies for selling Fuller Brushes for an hour, never really talking about journalism. When it was time for me to go, Trump assured me that I was just the kind of person cut out for Columbia, and he invited me to attend after I spent a year in law school.

I found law school intimidating. I did not like the large classes or the almost total absence of feedback. I was sufficiently afraid of failure that I studied hard, and slowly I began to do what generations before and after me have done: I began to "think like a lawyer." At the time I did not make much of the logical tool I had added to my arsenal, but my law training has been invaluable to me in my career—and in a very direct way served as the impetus for this book. As planned, after my first year of law school I enrolled in the journalism school, which I loved. It was the tumultuous fall of 1968, and I could not imagine a better place to be than Columbia, or a better thing to be doing there than studying journalism. *Not* as planned, I returned to law school after my year as a journalism student. My journalism teachers persuaded me that was a wise move, and it was, even though I have never actually practiced law. A few years after I graduated from law school, I got hired by the *New York Times.* It was my law degree, not my journalism credential, that the editors were most interested in. At the *Times,* I covered legal issues, and I spent a lot of time with lawyers. I began to see some of the similarities between lawyers and journalists more clearly, but I also began to see where they diverged.

Let me fast forward several decades to my second tour of duty at Columbia, this time as dean of the journalism school. My plan was not to stay long, and my mandate was to make some fundamental changes in the school during that short period. Very few faculty members at the school had ever earned tenure, and that had led to unwelcome turnover and poor morale. Journalism professors felt isolated from the other departments on campus. My job was to achieve some long-term stability by getting professors tenured. The university administration well understood the important public functions of the journalism school (it housed the *Columbia Journalism Review* and the Pulitzer Prizes), but most Columbia professors did not have a clue about what it meant for a major research university to have a journalism program. As is the custom in academic settings when change is warranted, a review of the school was held. Smart outsiders were brought in. In their tough-minded report (one member of the review team remarked how Columbia Journalism School had never innovated in *anything* in the past eighty years), the reviewers kept on repeating an image—citing how the school was walled off, physically, culturally, and intellectually, from the rest of the university. Those walls had to be knocked down.

That got me thinking even more about journalism's very real connections with other disciplines—connections I had long observed and attempted to strengthen. At Berkeley, where I had served as dean before coming to Columbia, I had taken steps to link up the journalism school with other units on campus. It seemed self-evident that journalists, who often relish being outsiders, had much to learn from other academic disciplines. Journalism surely fits within the larger framework of learning at a university: like the practitioners of any other discipline, journalists are at their best when they not only know what they know but also know how they know it. In other words, in the spirit of a university, journalists on campus should question the assumptions of their craft, and that is what I have tried to do in this book. In that sense, my attempts to strengthen the bond between journalists and those pursuing other fields became the genesis for this project.

The longer I stay in journalism, the more I recognize that it really is a collaborative field. It is unwise to go it alone. Journalists should know that they can turn to other fields for guidance—to law, to history, to economics, to the hard sciences. They are not alone in efforts to find, use, and interpret sources. No other discipline has a methodology that is a perfect fit with journalism. But there probably is no field that journalists cannot learn from.

The joy of teaching at a university is the steady influx of students, some of whom one gets to know well, and some of whom help in research, by doing hard work and by challenging a teacher's old-fashioned assumptions. In that regard, I wish to thank Kim-Mai Cutler and Nick Broten, who provided extraordinary help on this book. I am also indebted to two gifted editors, Rita Bernhard and Lawrence Grauman. And as the proximate cause of this book, I thank David Abrahamson of the Medill School of Journalism at Northwestern, the editor of this series. (Proximate cause is a useful legal concept, learned early in the first year of law school, in which an initial act sets off a sequence of events that are responsible for producing some concrete result.) With an uncommonly gentle touch, he had more confidence than I that I could actually finish this project.

Tom Goldstein

ONE

INTRODUCTION

No breach of faith in the recent history of journalism has measured up in size, scope, and audacity to the sins committed by Jayson Blair of the *New York Times* until his detection and forced resignation in 2003. There are many close contenders, and it surely should come as no surprise that a few rotten apples populate the barrel of journalists, just as there are at least a few rotten analysts and investors on Wall Street, a few public officials gone wrong, and some wayward doctors and lawyers.[1]

What concerns me in this book is not only that journalists lie, cheat, and make lots of mistakes. I am interested particularly in how journalists think about the idea of truth and how close they come to attaining it.

Blair's transgressions—stealing the words of others, putting words into other people's mouths, describing events and scenes as if he were an eyewitness when he was half a continent away—are nothing new in the field of journalism. Although Blair may have been far more audacious than his predecessors, many premier practitioners of the craft have long passed off fiction as fact, preying on a gullible and too-trusting public.

In the mid-eighteenth century, for instance, Samuel Johnson reported on the activities of the British Parliament for a publication called the *Gentlemen's Magazine* without ever attending the sessions. In his famous biography of Johnson, James Boswell wrote: "Johnson told me that as soon as he found out that the speeches were thought genuine, he determined that he would write no more of them." Shortly before his death, Johnson expressed regret to Boswell "for his having been the author of fictions, which had passed for realities."[2]

H. L. Mencken, early in his career, wrote a straight-faced newspaper column celebrating the seventy-fifth anniversary of the bathtub, in which he asserted with plausible historical detail that it had been invented in the 1840s, that Millard Fillmore when he was vice president had been the first to install one in the White House, that the medical profession and public had long regarded it with deep suspicion, and that laws had been passed against the perilous contraption by Virginia, Pennsylvania, and Massachusetts. This column, which appeared on a news page above a short item about a service fraternity planning a "war services board," was, it turned out, made up.[3] Mencken was astonished to find his little joke had been taken at face value. He was still more astonished to find newspapers and magazines copying these "facts" in ever-widening circles, so that they cropped up year after year in the most dignified periodicals.[4]

This incident is recalled by Allan Nevins, who began his career as a newspaperman and then became a leading historian at Columbia University, where he wrote of the Civil War and of American business history. Part of Nevins's book *The Gateway to History* was excerpted in *The Historian as Detective,* a delightful collection assembled by Robin Winks of Yale University, who ruminated on the validity of different types of evidence. "The historian knows just how fallible his daily paper may be (although there are many who seem to feel that they cannot be certain whether it is raining or snowing until the *New York Times* has told them so)," Winks wrote, "and so he is doubly conscious of the errors of fact, as well as of the distortions of opinion and the misquotations of authority, that lie in wait for the unwary researcher in nineteenth-century sheets, in an age when journalism was yellow, as they say, as well as red, white and blue."[5]

In 1920, noted journalists Walter Lippmann and Charles Merz published a long essay in the *New Republic* examining press coverage of the Russian Revolution of 1917.[6] This study showed that American papers gave their readers an account of the revolution that, in Christopher Lasch's words, was "distorted by anti-Bolshevik prejudices, wishful thinking and sheer ignorance."[7]

The highs and lows of journalism were captured in *The Front Page*—first the play and then the assorted movies, which became sentimental favorites among journalists of a certain vintage. First staged in 1928, *The Front Page* includes a raucous scene where journalists invent the news and ignore what happens before their eyes—a comedic situation meant to suggest more than a passing resemblance to Chicago journalism of that era.

In 1961, Alastair Reid, a well-regarded poet and reporter for the *New Yorker,* described Spaniards in a small, flyblown bar openly jeering a television speech by Francisco Franco.[8] But the bar had been shut for years, and Reid was using literary license in order to reach, for him at least, a larger truth. Reid's embellishment, when it became known nearly a quarter century later, became front-page news in the *Wall Street Journal* and the *New York Times.* The guardians of the press pilloried him for his infraction and wondered what had happened to the vaunted standards of the *New Yorker.*

As other sins of journalists became known over time, suggestions for reform were offered by some of the most provocative and well-intentioned thinkers about the press. In *The Brass Check,* in 1920, Upton Sinclair proposed that a law be enacted forbidding newspapers from publishing interviews without first having received approval from the interviewees. No one paid much attention to this suggestion, or to other proposals, such as establishing municipally owned newspapers, advanced by Sinclair.

A. J. Liebling, the incomparable critic, told the story of how Albert Camus, once the editor of *Combat,* a resistance newspaper published in Paris during World War II, had whimsically proposed the creation of a "control" newspaper that would appear one hour after the others with estimates of the percentage of truth in each of their stories, and with pieces interpreting how the stories may have been slanted. This is how Camus explained his idea: "We'd have complete dossiers on the interests, policies and idiosyncrasies of the owners. Then we'd have a dossier on every journalist in the world. The interest, prejudices, and quirks of the owner would equal Z. The prejudices, quirks, and private interests of the journalist, Y. Z times Y would give you X, the probable amount of truth in the story." Camus never got around to testing this scheme. His energies, Liebling deadpanned, were "dissipated" in creative writing.[9]

In a marvelous essay published in the *Yale Review* in 1980, John Hersey, equally skilled in fiction and nonfiction, noted that "the minute a writer offers 998 out of 1,000 facts, the worm of bias has begun to wriggle. The vision of each witness is particular. Tolstoy pointed out that immediately after a battle there are as many remembered versions of it as there have been participants." Even so, Hersey continued, the merging of fiction and fact in reporting was not acceptable. The one "sacred" rule of journalism, he said, is: "The writer must not invent. The legend on the license must read: NONE OF THIS WAS MADE UP."[10] The "ethics of journalism," Hersey wrote, "must be based on the simple truth that every journalist knows the difference between the distortion that comes from subtracting observed data and the distortion that comes from adding invented data."[11]

In 1983, Abe Raskin, the distinguished *New York Times* writer and editor who spent many of his later years worrying about the press, asked: "Does the proliferation of journalism forms, ranging from straight news reporting through a sometimes bewildering assortment of analytic, entertainment and gossip columns, require notice to the public that varying gradations of credence ought to be applied to the varying types of news treatment?"[12]

As odious, breathtaking, or frivolous as the transgressions have been, and as inventive, high-minded, or harebrained as the proposed solutions have seemed, it is this type of untruth—the fabrication, the lying—that has long preoccupied journalists. In the fall of 1980, an article by a twenty-six-year-old reporter at the *Washington Post* named Janet Cooke electrified Washington. She wrote movingly of an eight-year-old heroin addict in a story called "Jimmy's World."[13] The following spring, she was awarded a Pulitzer Prize, and the story immediately unraveled. "Jimmy" turned out be a composite, and the touching quotes attributed to the boy were made up. Cooke confessed, "There is no Jimmy," after she was fired. The *Post* returned the Pulitzer Prize awarded for the story.[14] Ben Bradlee, the steely and debonair editor of the *Post,* recalled in his memoir, *A Good Life,* "The possibility that the story was not true never entered my head."[15] The *Post,* in the words of its chairman, Katharine Graham, took a "terrible drubbing" for having published the fraudulent article.[16]

Journalism has not necessarily learned its lesson from "Jimmy's World" and similar debacles. Judging by reported incidents, instances of fraud in American journalism appear to be growing.

Or perhaps not. Aided by technology, our mechanisms for

detecting such frauds may have improved, just in the way we have observed an alarming increase in the incidence of peanut allergies, particularly among the young, in part because we have become more adept at detecting such allergies.

Still, we are simply not able to quantify whether journalists are getting better, or worse, at behaving well and telling the truth. It is a well-worn and damaging complaint against journalism that subjects of articles know that when articles are written about them or about something they were involved with, they are usually wrong. This observation is an old one. The modern version of the complaint can be traced to John Gordon, the editor of the *Sunday Express* in Great Britain, who in July 1946 sent a message on accuracy to his sub-editors and reporters, remarking: "I do not wish to be hypercritical, but the plain fact is—and we all know it to be true—that whenever we see a story in a newspaper concerning something we know about, it is more often wrong than right."[17] Gordon's message was repeated in the 1949 report of the Royal Commission on the Press, which had been charged with furthering the free expression of opinion and ensuring the greatest practicable accuracy in the presentation of the news. The Gordon quote also appeared in *The Sugar Pill* by T. S. Matthews, a former editor of *Time* magazine who criticized the press for manufacturing "all the big news it can,"[18] and it was repeated by the author and teacher Penn Kimball in a 1963 essay entitled "Journalism: Art, Craft or Profession?" In Kimball's view, reporters must learn to master "two opposite psychological states." One is the capacity to become immersed in stories they are sent to cover. The other is to remain detached from "these same intense involvements, to stand outside the experience and place it in perspective for the reader."[19]

The observation that John Gordon was attempting to make, of

course, has been repeated countless times since, although its connection to its British originator is usually lost. The Royal Commission, in its quaint way, discussed with keen understanding the second-hand nature of news, underscoring the tension between truth and journalism and explaining why journalistic truth is necessarily not the entire truth:

> A daily newspaper can seldom be certain of its facts in the sense, for example, in which a nautical almanac is certain of its facts . . . news is too ephemeral to acquire the authenticity conferred by investigation and proof. A daily newspaper is obliged by the character of its material to treat as ascertained facts pieces of information of widely differing reliability. Much of its information is obtained by one fallible human being from another, usually by word of mouth. If the informant himself is reliable, he may be misunderstood by a journalist unfamiliar with his technicalities or with points which to the expert are too obvious to mention; if the informant is not certain of his facts, he may mislead the journalist. Even an eyewitness's account may be untrustworthy, particularly if the witness is a member of the public not trained to observe accurately and tells his story in an atmosphere of excitement. Not all news reports come from one person or from people in a position to know the truth, and when the sources are many and indirect the risks of inaccuracy are multiplied.[20]

The last observation that the Royal Commission made—about the importance of sources and their relationship to journalistic truth—is one that has preoccupied journalists for years, and rarely has there been a satisfactory explanation of what journalists should do when their sources are faulty.

In a postmortem to "Jimmy's World," the National News Council (which very quietly dissolved itself in 1984) examined what went wrong at the *Washington Post*. Ben Bradlee, in an interview with members of the council, asserted that "the truth is not something that can be grasped."[21] He went on to say that measuring journalistic truth was an inexact science and that just tightening up on the use of sources was but a limited answer. "When the President is lying, you are lying," he observed. For him, the most interesting revelation in the Pentagon Papers—the chronicle of U.S. involvement in the Vietnam War—was its disclosure that his friend, Secretary of Defense Robert McNamara, had told President Lyndon Johnson in a private White House conference that the military position in Vietnam was deteriorating rapidly—a statement, Bradlee said, that McNamara "made only 20 minutes after painting a rosy picture of the situation for reporters who met him at Andrews Air Force Base."[22]

If journalists are routinely lied to, was First Amendment lawyer and professor Jane Kirtley correct in defending the press, which had prematurely accused Richard Jewell in 1996 of setting off a bomb in a park in Atlanta near the Olympics? "We cannot be the guarantors of the truth of what government says," Kirtley stated on *Crossfire,* the now-defunct CNN show where two advocates would take opposite sides of an issue to arouse the audience—and presumably arrive at the truth. "We can only report as accurately as we can what the government says," Kirtley continued, echoing Ben Bradlee's view. "The press is not bound by the rules of evidence, for example, and they're not required to meet the same standards that a prosecutor would have to meet in court before they go with a story, but of course they have to be as accurate as they possibly can."[23]

In this light, was Judith Miller's apology for her misleading reports in the *New York Times* on the causes of the Iraq War necessary—or sufficient? "W.M.D.—I got it totally wrong," said

Miller. "The analysts, the experts and the journalists who covered them—we were all wrong. If your sources are wrong, you are wrong. I did the best job that I could."[24]

In other words, should or can we expect journalism to be no more than stenographically accurate? Or is journalism only an aspect of a postmodern sensibility that accepts the impossibility of determining the truth? Shouldn't we expect more? Of course we should.

* * *

As a society, we are better equipped than ever to distinguish fact-based truth from the sham, but often we seem no longer to care very much about making the distinction. Contemporary journalism has played a supporting role in the eroding influence of fact-based truth. Journalism, as a central foundation of our culture, needs to do a much better job of achieving literal accuracy and, when appropriate, explaining with greater insight why the quest for literal accuracy cannot always be achieved.

For many of the past twenty-two years, I have taught a large lecture course on understanding the media. Among the texts I routinely assign are two modern nonfiction classics, Walter Lippmann's *Public Opinion* and Daniel Boorstin's *The Image*. Lippmann's *Public Opinion* is an examination of the role citizens play in a democracy and how the press shapes democratic thought, and Boorstin's *The Image* examines how hype can distort our appreciation of public affairs. Each year, in writing and talking about these books, many students refer to them as "novels." I cringe, then I correct the students until my face turns red, but the misunderstanding keeps cropping up. This is disheartening, but it is no longer surprising. These are smart students. They either do not know or do not care about the distinction between fact and fiction.

For a while, early in 2006, it seemed that no one except nitpickers cared whether James Frey's fabricated personal memoir, *A Million Little Pieces,* was true or not. He had made up significant parts of the book, passing off fiction as fact. It is not easy to know what to expect from a memoir these days—whether it belongs to literature, or history, or journalism, or all of them. Initially, Frey was not held to the standard of accuracy required in other kinds of nonfiction. What was important, said Oprah Winfrey, an early promoter of Frey's in a phone call to Larry King, was the larger truth of Frey's book. Then a backlash set in, and Winfrey flogged Frey on her show only days after she had championed him. She apologized for having defended Frey and in so doing leaving "the impression that the truth does not matter."[25]

The impulse to improve on reality that was evident in Frey's self-aggrandizing memoir of drug addiction is similar to the impulse evident in the memorable instances of journalistic misdeeds committed by Jayson Blair and Janet Cooke. They, too, lied and fabricated as they sought a more dramatic version of reality. That impulse is also evident in the docudrama, a hybrid format of unusual staying power on network television as well as feature-length movies. Starting a generation or so ago, the general public began to gain much of their understanding of current events from docudramas—rather than from journalism or history books. *All the President's Men* tells of the fall of a president. *The Right Stuff* re-creates the early days of the National Aeronautics and Space Administration (NASA). *The Killing Fields* is based on the escape from Cambodia of Dith Pran, the loyal assistant to *New York Times* reporter Sydney Schanberg. *Silkwood* relates the mysterious death of the whistleblower in a nuclear power plant. *And the Band Played On* chronicles the early years of the AIDS epidemic. Countless shows, mostly on television, have portrayed members of the

Kennedy clan. One of them, *Marilyn and Bobby: Her Final Affair,* broke new ground in "docudrama shamelessness," wrote Richard Zoglin in *Time* magazine.[26]

The genre has uncommon durability. In the fall of 2006, the powerful movie *The Queen* portrayed Queen Elizabeth and her response to the death of Princess Diana. Actors and actresses played royalty. Diana, a major character in the movie, was represented by actual television clips. Weeks after the movie premiered, a two-hour documentary, *The Queen at 80,* aired on BBC America. As in the movie, Prime Minister Tony Blair visited the queen in her chambers. (Permission was granted to film the *real* Tony Blair and the *real* Queen Elizabeth.) As in the movie, the queen's relationship with Princess Diana was examined. In a dizzying mix of reality and fiction, some of the commercials that were shown during the TV documentary advertised the movie, featuring short clips of the fictional Tony Blair and the fictional Queen Elizabeth.

A major controversy over docudramas erupted over the television special *The Path to 9/11,* a distorted rendering of the most significant event of the young century shown five years after the attacks on the World Trade Center. In portraying the government's failure to prevent the attacks, the five-hour docudrama contained invented scenes, characters, and dialogue. The most questionable scenes alleged that members of the Clinton administration were negligent, even though this charge was not supported by the findings of the 9/11 Commission that investigated the events. In response to protests, ABC did make last-minute changes that removed some of the most egregious distortions.

While a documentary is supposed to maintain strict fidelity to facts, docudramas blend fact and fiction, presumably to shed light on essential truths. In a docudrama, literal truth—whether two people had a specific conversation, for example—yields to a presumably broader truth—did one of these people betray the other? Viewers therefore are put on notice that what they are watching is not necessarily accurate. The buildings and landscape may be real, whereas the players are only actors. But judging from the high ratings of docudramas and the low ratings of documentaries, people are not terribly concerned about literal truth.

In fact, literal truth has no legal standing. Docudramas received an important legal blessing nearly twenty years ago from a federal judge in New York who established First Amendment protections for the genre. That case involved a libel suit arising out of the movie *Missing*, a political drama that was directed by Constantin Costa-Gavras and set in Chile at a time when it was in the throes of a military coup. An American activist disappeared and presumably was killed during the brutal coup. Federal Judge Milton Pollack ruled that altering facts was legally acceptable if the docudrama makers did not entertain "serious doubts of the truth of the essence of the telescoped composite."[27] Nonetheless, the term "docudrama" is an oxymoron, and the format can be dangerous. Max Frankel, the former executive editor of the *New York Times* and a fierce critic of docudramas, once observed, "To blur the distinction between fact and drama is to blur the journalistic enterprise."[28]

No matter how strenuous or penetrating the criticism, docudramas proliferate. The pattern is the same. Critics condemn a forthcoming docudrama for playing around with reality. Critics register major consternation. The docudrama is televised or screened. And the controversy is soon forgotten. It is as if the public's appetite for mixing fact and fiction cannot be sated.

In the future, it is quite possible that journalism will further loosen its grip on the truth. Although journalists continue to see their jobs as collecting and verifying information as best they can before disseminating it, the Internet may increasingly accommodate a public demand for unverified information. Richard Siklos, who has reported on press issues for many years, noted that news organizations that rely on standards of ethics, accuracy, and expertise—however imperfect the implementation—are "now wrestling with the unsettling notion of sharing the digital page with anyone who wants to weigh in on their work."[29] Many bloggers say they at least sometimes try to verify facts before posting them on their websites. Their essential approach, however, is to offer a space for all to post what they know or think.[30]

For bloggers, truth is created collectively, not through a hierarchy of fact seekers and verifiers. Information is not necessarily vetted before it is disseminated; instead, it is distributed via multiple and usually undifferentiated views. This is a different kind of truth than the truth that journalists have become accustomed to, arrived at by different means. Truth, in the bloggers' view, emerges from the discourse.[31]

★ ★ ★

I am interested in you, I tell students in my lecture course. I am interested in what you think of me. I want to know. How do I find out? This is the scenario I pose in my class. I can be an eyewitness. I can look at your faces—your sneers, your grins. I can see imaginary lightbulbs pop over your heads, or I can see your eyelids droop as you doze off. Or, like many journalists, I could take another approach and ask probing questions. If I had the time and skill, I could take a survey. I could bring in experts to make a judgment. If I wanted to push the limits of ethics, I could go incognito and overhear your conversations to capture unvarnished responses. Or, for the sake of this hypothetical, I could call on my friend the prosecutor and have him compel you to testify under oath. These days, I suppose, I could look at self-descriptions on MySpace or Facebook.

In this book I outline many of the traditional ways that journalists attempt to arrive at truth and then analyze how some of these time-honored conventions may actually work against finding truth. Journalists, for instance, talk to sources in person or on the phone. Typically they do not read books or analyze data. They work under time pressure. "Go with what you've got"—the signature admonition of John Hohenberg, a longtime professor at the Columbia University Graduate School of Journalism—suggests the hurried and incomplete nature of much of journalism.

As objectivity fades from the journalist's lexicon, fairness and balance have become the new slogans. Most journalists go to extremes to demonstrate balance—even if the underlying facts clearly point in one direction. But balancing opposing statements will not necessarily yield truth, which rarely has two sides in the way, for example, that CNN's *Crossfire* presented issues. In an oversimplification, this is how some journalists seeking balance work: One hundred international experts rejected the theory that exercise might cause farsightedness, but one local legislator, with a background as a truck driver, called the issue "still disputed." By giving equal weight to the legislator, the reporter portrays the situation inaccurately, unwittingly suggesting that "journalistic 'balance' is synonymous with accuracy."[32] Balance can be a false goal, not only for journalists. As Jonathan Cole, the former provost of Columbia University, wrote in *Daedalus:* "We should remember that the proper goal of higher education is enlightenment—not some abstract ideal of 'balance.'"[33]

Journalists live by a set of conventions that they use to "reassure themselves that if they have not quite reached the truth, they are certainly nearing its backdoor," wrote Deni Elliott, a specialist in media ethics and the founder of the Ethics Center at the University of Montana, in an essay on "journalistic truth."[34] Elliott listed four such conventions, which may be summarized as follows:

1. Sources with important titles or familiar names have probably been used repeatedly, and so their views are safely presented as true.
2. The same information that comes from two independent sources is usually safe to present as truth.
3. Sources who have few conflicts of interest are generally more reliable than sources with more conflicts. Sources with few or no conflicts are considered to be more independent.
4. Documents are the most reliable sort of evidence. They do not lie.[35]

Elliott's list is illustrative and could surely be expanded and developed. For instance, in a later chapter, I discuss why one of the enduring taboos of journalists—checkbook journalism, or paying sources for information—should be reexamined.

Writing this book has made me very self-conscious. In one chapter I note that in Janet Malcolm's books about journalists, lawyers, and biographers, she may really be writing about herself. I wonder if that applies to me and whether I am guilty of some of the very things that I complain about. In this book, for instance, I quote many people—a practice that critics are concerned about in journalism. In *The Art of Fact: A Historical Anthology of Literary Journalism,* Kevin Kerrane and Ben Yagoda criticized the time-honored journalistic convention of using quotes as "antiliterary" and wondered if journalists use quotes to "help cover your posterior: if someone else provides the information, you don't have to stand by it."[36] Reporters can verify what Jones said, even if they cannot be sure of what Jones knew. Relying on sources becomes something of a hedge. As John Soloski of the University of Georgia wrote, "then sources and not journalists are responsible for the accuracy of the facts."[37]

Using, or overusing, identified sources presents one set of problems. Using anonymous sources presents a different set of problems, those having to do with credibility. But journalists abandon the use of anonymous sources at their peril. "The cost of relying only on on-the-record sources would be the loss of a tremendous amount of news, much of it far more accurate and important than the pablum delivered in press releases and on the-record news conferences," wrote James Stewart, an author and teacher.[38] Stewart, like Deni Elliott, questioned the magic formula of needing two sources to confirm a fact. "The two-source rule championed by the *Washington Post* in the Watergate era—or any other hard and fast rule of that nature—has always struck me as nonsense," he wrote. Far more important than the number of sources is who those sources are and how close they are to the information they are imparting. At the same time, Stewart wrote, in a book review, "it is a truism that more sources are always better, and relying on a single source requires a degree of caution that is in scant evidence at many organizations."[39]

In sum, it is critical for at least two reasons that we understand how well journalism succeeds in meeting standards of accuracy. First, journalism has become a standard against which other genres are compared. Memoirists, for instance, may not owe the readers the same record of accuracy that newspaper reporters do, but memoirists should not (as James Frey did) fabricate experiences. The second reason is that journalism is a foundation of our culture. It becomes the basis for history. To summarily dismiss journalism merely as the first rough draft of history (as Philip Graham of the *Washington Post* famously did) lets journalism off too easily. It needs more rigor and more responsibility.

In this book, I look to other disciplines, such as history and law, in order to better understand journalistic truth. Journalists need to refine their techniques by learning and appreciating how other people in other disciplines go about their work. To be sure, the journalist's attempt to seek out and report the truth is unlike the mathematician's quest for abstract truth or the scientist's search for principles that can be generalized. But even the hard sciences, and surely the soft sciences, have relevance to journalism. An observation from Elizabeth Loftus, a psychologist, for example, is surely relevant: she has spent her professional life studying the fallibility of human memory in an effort to "dispel the myth that human memory is infallible and immune from distortion."[40] In her quest to grasp the accuracy of memory, she has made a career of testifying to the unreliability of eyewitness testimony. Because journalists rely on eyewitness reporting at least some of the time, they should be aware of the latest thinking on eyewitness testimony from a psychological perspective.

However, the press, as Jane Kirtley noted, is not bound by the same rules of evidence that govern a criminal dispute, and a journalist, thankfully, is not required to meet the same burden of proof expected of a prosecutor in court. Nor do journalists have the many tools that prosecutors have to help them uncover the truth. But looking closely at the justice system can shed light on how journalists operate.

Truth is a relatively recent concept for journalism, compared to other disciplines. Fabrication was a fixture of journalism for much of the nineteenth and twentieth centuries. "The thought that news reports should be true dawned on journalists only recently," wrote Jack Fuller in the opening page of *News Values,* which traces the idea of objectivity to a group of people who were seeking legitimacy in an era of scientific discovery.[41] In *The Elements of Journalism,* Bill Kovach and Tom Rosenstiel observed that journalists in the latter part of the nineteenth century talked about something called "realism," not objectivity. "This was the idea," the authors noted, "that if reporters simply dug out the facts and ordered them together, the truth would reveal itself rather naturally." They added, however, that at the beginning of the twentieth century "some journalists began to worry about the naiveté of realism." In part, with the rise of propaganda and the enhanced role of press agents, journalism was changing.[42]

Journalists, too, were developing a greater recognition of human subjectivity. Walter Lippmann's contribution to this debate was his observation in the early 1920s that news and truth are not the same and overlap only infrequently, where results are definite and measurable, such as the scores of baseball games or the outcomes of elections.[43] (In this observation, Lippmann was echoing H. L. Mencken, who had noted several years earlier that he knew of "no subject, in truth, save perhaps baseball, on which the average American newspaper, even in the larger cities, discourses with unfailing sense and understanding."[44]) The early 1900s saw the emergence of objective reporting, a routine that was meant to emulate the scientific method as closely as possible. For journalists this meant interviews with sources, ordinarily official sources with strong credentials. It meant juxtaposing conflicting truth-claims, where certain contentions were reported as "fact" regardless of their validity.[45]

Just what "truth" might be and how best to arrive at it, however, became increasingly difficult to define from the twentieth century's beginning to its end. Just as journalism began to embrace objectivity, other disciplines were beginning to question its utility. In an important insight, Jane Singer of the University of Iowa noted in a conference paper that the intellectual world was largely abandoning the notion of truth as something that could be perceived and rationally verified, just as journalists were embracing that notion.[46]

* * *

Journalism, of course, has changed dramatically over the years, and it continues to change at a fast pace. The gates to journalism have opened wide, embracing many more activities than they did when I started covering elementary school graduations as a reporter at the *Buffalo Evening News* in the summers of the late 1960s. We need to keep asking what news is. News may be defined as what's important or interesting, and preferably both. News is relative in that it depends on which audience the news organization is trying to reach. The *New York Times,* with its highly educated and affluent readership, has one audience. But it also has an impact beyond its circulation number because it greatly influences other decision makers. It is the most closely scrutinized and emulated newspaper in the world. The *San Francisco Chronicle,* with its highly educated but more eccentric readership, has a different audience. The *Wall Street Journal* appeals to those interested in business and finance. Television seeks a mass audience. The Internet opens uncharted territory for targeted, niche journalism and for the spread of information that may not be fully verified. Several years ago, I taught a seminar with Max Frankel, who had recently retired from the *New York Times.* Here are some of the questions we asked students to think about:

- Can we define news better than Supreme Court Justice Potter Stewart defined obscenity when he declared, "I know it when I see it"?
- The crash of a commercial airliner is news. A safe landing is not, unless the plane was hijacked or otherwise crippled. Why does bad news crowd out the good?
- A gang rape in Central Park is big news in New York. A rape in a Bronx elevator is small news. Rape in a rural haystack is hardly worth a mention. Why is the morality of news so selective?
- Why does the news of conflict crowd out the news of cooperation? Why do crime and sports get more attention than science and literature? Why do spectacle and photography so often take precedence in the news over information? Or should we learn to understand spectacle as a kind of information? Why do our eyes and emotions define news more often than our intellect does?
- How should we rate the news of outside events against the news we make or discover by ourselves?
- Why do we care where the famous eat and sleep? And why are they newsworthy in the first place?
- What happens to news as it ages, from the instantaneous to the daily, the weekly, the annually, and the historic? What happens to news as it shifts from the neighborhood to the region, the natural environment, the globe, and the universe? Should recent news trump previous news? Must news focus on "today" and "yesterday"? Should nearer news trump the distant?

Our class did not come up with any definitive answers to those questions, but we began to think of the essence of news—and it is a quest for this essence that I pursue in the chapters that follow. In deciding what news is, we may in fact be at a cultural divide, and in that light, the 2004 presidential election may be seen as a turning point in how we view the news. Shortly before the election, *Time* magazine ran a probing cover story, "Who Owns the Truth?" Members of Swift Boat Veterans for Truth challenged several aspects of Democratic candidate John F. Kerry's military record, in addition to his account of the March 13, 1969, mission for which he was awarded the Bronze Star. Kerry's accusers may have raised serious doubts about his war record in many quarters, but they failed to come up with sufficient evidence to prove him a liar. Kerry was outraged that the surrogates of a president who had not fought in Vietnam questioned his heroism, but once the charges had entered the national conversation, he could not shake them.

"Old media and their insurgent competitors are locked in an asymmetrical conflict, with one set of outlets following the traditional conventions of neutrality and balanced coverage and the other not," wrote Nancy Gibbs of *Time.* "So when the talk shows began covering the charges, they adhered to those conventions and gave equal time to those leveling the attacks and the Kerry representatives disputing them."[47]

Weeks earlier, the difference between the new and old ways of looking at news and truth was encapsulated in a conversation, quite lengthy for television, on *Nightline* between its host, Ted Koppel, and Jon Stewart of the *Daily Show.* In the spirit of a TV show of this sort, the conversation, which aired on September 3, 2004, is disjointed in spots, with Koppel and Stewart uttering incomplete thoughts and interrupting each other. But through the extended conversation they convey a sense of the tension between news and truth and question whether a reporter has a greater responsibility than just to transcribe what someone in authority has to say.

Jon Stewart

The swift boat guys. They are making things up. It's there—
the public record is all in John Kerry's favor in this. . . . Yet, there
is this moral equivalency of their story and his story. The burden
has been put on him to disprove something that happened thirty-
five years ago, [something] that is in the public record, because
these guys have come out. In that moment, it seems to me that
the public should care. . . . I can only walk up to that line. I can
only point at it and go, "Ooh, ah, ah." But . . . I don't have the
credibility.

Ted Koppel

You're doing the dancing monkey thing again.

Jon Stewart

But I don't have the credibility to be able to say—I can only
do it in joke form. Which, by the way, I'm fine with.

Then Koppel suggests that candidate Kerry bore some responsibility for his predicament because it was he who began his campaign
by proclaiming: "John Kerry reporting for duty." And it was
Kerry who was surrounded by his "band of brothers" at every
public appearance. Then Stewart takes a different tack.

Jon Stewart

I believe that right now the media rewards which team plays
the game better. In other words, when people are saying,
"George Bush is going to win," what they're not saying is, "He
is the better man with the better policy and is giving the American public an honest description of what he is going to do." What
the people are saying is, "These guys are good. They are playing
this game like masters, like maestros. They are conducting this
election with such expertise." . . .

Ted Koppel

I think you're arguing about the difference between fact and truth, which is the great problem with journalism. . . .

Jon Stewart

Fact and truth? Are you going to tell me the Holocaust didn't happen?

Ted Koppel

For the sake of argument, let's say President Bush comes out there Thursday night and out of the blue talks about that well-known drug dealer and pedophile, Ted Koppel . . . and then my colleagues the next morning say the president of the United States last night, in a surprising diversion from the rest of his speech, accused ABC host Ted Koppel of being a pedophile and a drug dealer. Are they factually correct in reporting that the president of the United States said that? Is it news that he said that? Sure, it is. Is it the truth? No. The truth may not emerge until . . .

Jon Stewart

We'll be right back. Tomorrow on *Nightline,* Ted Koppel's resignation.

Ted Koppel

Come back here. Come back here, Stewart. But do you get my point? There is a difference between facts which are reported immediately. . . . It's a fact that these—that these veterans were in Vietnam. They themselves were on the swift boats. They are saying these things. The truth may not catch up for another week or two or six. But in the meantime . . .

Jon Stewart

But they're explaining the vulnerability in the system. . . .

Ted Koppel

That's exactly right.[48]

For Stewart, the media has to be more aggressive and not be satisfied to wait, as Koppel said, for the truth to "catch up for another week or two or six." Journalists, in other words, must dig beneath the surface for truth and not merely repeat the lies and misstatements of others.

---◆---

TWO

JOURNALISM AS
NONREPRESENTATIVE TRUTH

On February 27, 1992, Stella Liebeck, then seventy-nine years old, sat in a fully stopped car to remove the lid of the coffee she had purchased for forty-nine cents at a McDonald's drive-thru window in Albuquerque, New Mexico. She wanted to add cream and sugar. Seated on the passenger side of a Ford Probe driven by her grandson, she placed the Styrofoam coffee cup between her legs to free up both her hands so that she could pry off the lid. As she did so, the cup tipped, spilling all the coffee into her lap, where it was rapidly soaked up into her sweatpants. She screamed in pain.[1]

The grandson proceeded to drive out of the parking lot, until, a minute later, his grandmother became quite nauseated. He headed for the nearest hospital emergency room, which was full, and then made his way to a second hospital, where Liebeck was admitted. The coffee had been scalding—it was served at between 180 and 190 degrees Fahrenheit—and Liebeck suffered extensive third-degree burns on her thighs, buttocks, genitals, and groin area. Hospitalized for a week, she was permanently disfigured, temporarily disabled, and subjected to a series of painful skin grafts.

What followed catapulted Liebeck into a prominence she did not seek or want. She sued McDonald's for serving excessively hot coffee and soon became famous as a personification of the greedy plaintiff. On one level, her case came to represent a dysfunctional justice system, and the reporting of her plight raised important issues of how civil justice gets reported. On a deeper level, the case raised the familiar question of what constitutes news. The reporting of the story also indicated that journalists could do their jobs better if they were aware of the tools of other disciplines and applied them to their work.

Before her accident with the coffee, Liebeck, a recently retired department store salesclerk and member of a longtime Republican family, had never filed a lawsuit. In a letter, she asked McDonald's to reevaluate the temperature to which it heated its coffee. She acknowledged that she was responsible for the accident, but she felt that the coffee was too hot. She wanted to be compensated for medical expenses not covered by Medicare up to $20,000. After six months, McDonald's offered her $800. (In the previous decade, it turned out, the company had dealt with 700 similar complaints and had paid out nearly $750,000, which averages out to a bit more than $1,000 a claim.)

After a trial that lasted seven days, the jury spent only four hours to reach a verdict favorable to Liebeck. The jury awarded her $160,000 in compensatory damages and $2.7 million in punitive damages, but the judge reduced the total award to $640,000. On November 30, 1994, instead of pursuing the case further, McDonald's settled with Stella Liebeck for an undisclosed sum. Although the initial lawsuit received extensive coverage, the reduction of the jury's award and the final settlement were barely reported on. Indeed, no journalist was present at the trial, and the posttrial maneuverings were scarcely covered. The public, therefore, generally was left with the erroneous impression that Liebeck had won millions of dollars for something she had done to herself, even though lawsuits of this type often end in settlements or with reduced monetary awards.

Stories like hers, about an out-of-control justice system, are a staple of American popular culture. Her story became almost mythic, Thomas F. Burke wrote in *Lawyers, Lawsuits, and Legal Rights: The Battle over Litigation in American Society,* radiating "through public discourse because it illustrated what 'everyone knows'—that Americans routinely sue others for accidents they themselves are responsible for, that big corporations are excessively punished because they are 'big pockets' and that tort plaintiffs are overcompensated by runaway juries. Indeed, aspects of the Stella Liebeck story that were inconvenient to this portrayal—such as the fact that Liebeck settled for roughly one-fifth of the widely publicized $2.9 million jury verdict, that her burns were horrifyingly severe, or that McDonald's coffee had previously scalded hundreds—were widely ignored."[2]

The press was brutal to her. The *San Diego Union-Tribune* called the "absurd judgment" a "stunning illustration of what is wrong with America's civil justice system."[3] The *Oakland Tribune* editorialized: "The poster woman for this sort of ludicrous lawsuit is an 81-year-old New Mexico woman who sued McDonald's after she spilled her hot McDonald's coffee in her lap. . . . Is there any doubt in anyone's mind that our legal system is being badly abused? Greedy lawyers, victims out to make a buck and a culture that encourages people to sue instead of accepting their own responsibility for working things out have closed with cases that don't belong there."[4] In short order, Liebeck became an important political symbol. In 1997, five years after she was burned, she was used by both sides in the battle over efforts to protect manufacturers from excessive liability claims and to cap the amount that persons could receive in damages.[5]

But this was just another battle in a long-standing conflict that began in the 1970s, when insurance companies, tobacco interests, and large industry launched a political campaign for tort reform that would, ostensibly, limit the number of what they considered frivolous lawsuits. These lawsuits, they said, clogged the courts, raised insurance costs, and produced exorbitant or unmerited awards. By framing their cause as "reform," those seeking to change the status quo had a distinct rhetorical advantage. The tort reform movement found willing allies among conservative politicians. Vice President Dan Quayle, in a major speech in 1991 before the American Bar Association, estimated that tort litigation cost over $300 billion each year and labeled the civil justice system a "self-inflicted competitive disadvantage" for America.[6] And in Tenet Nine of the 1994 Contract with America, Republicans promised that if they took control of Congress, changing the civil justice system would be their prime objective.

Arrayed against the tort reformers was an alliance of plaintiffs' trial lawyers and consumer groups who argued that they were trying to defend the right of people to seek redress in courts.[7] They saw the expansion of torts rights in the post–World War II era as a progressive change. Judges, they said, were recognizing that landowners, doctors, and manufacturers should take responsibility for harm they had done to the public.

Business interests painted the trial lawyers as piranhas, feeding off society for their own financial gain. Lawyers and consumer groups, in turn, portrayed business leaders as greedy fat cats who wanted to enrich themselves at the expense of American consumers. In the heat of the legislative battle, the business side broadcast a radio commercial denouncing the monetary award initially granted to Liebeck as the height of absurdity. The trial lawyers and various consumer groups argued that the commercial was a quintessential example of how big business distorted the debate. Public Citizen, a consumer advocate group, brought Liebeck to a Capitol Hill news conference to describe the details of her case.

In the coverage of the Liebeck case, the journalistic reality differed from the legal reality, the final outcome of the McDonald's lawsuit. Because the facts were not well or widely reported, the public was left to see this case as another example of outrageous behavior by plaintiffs and their lawyers. In their important book *Distorting the Law,* William Haltom and Michael McCann concluded that "readers of the press, even very careful readers, would have no reason to doubt claims of the litigation explosion over the last two decades."[8]

Haltom, a professor in the Department of Politics and Government at the University of Puget Sound, and McCann, director of the Comparative and Society Studies Center at the University of Washington, Seattle, examined coverage of civil lawsuits in the *New York Times,* the *Wall Street Journal,* the *Washington Post,* the *Los Angeles Times,* and the *Christian Science Monitor* from 1980 to 1999 and offered impressive documentation that "anyone who relies on these five papers or on media that count on these five will be barraged by extravagant numbers out of line with routine real-world accounts."[9] In other words, "Ordinary news coverage has supported and encouraged another basic premise of tort reform: plaintiffs seem to be litigating, especially against business, not only with great frequency but also with inordinate success. News narratives seem to bear out the familiar lore that plaintiffs routinely win suits that they should lose or should never file."[10]

From their findings, Halton and McCann concluded that journalists "skimp" on details that complicate a case and unwittingly convey the messages of those who call themselves tort reformers "with minimal or no investigation and criticism."[11] The authors, like many serious researchers before them, refuted the common wisdom. They documented how litigation is not exploding at all, that Americans are not particularly litigious, and that juries, in fact, typically favor business. In a review of their book, Michael Schudson, a distinguished sociologist, explained that the academic consensus is well documented: "Almost all 'law and society' sociologists, anthropologists, political scientists and law professors agree that the litigation explosion is largely a myth."[12] Key facts get lost in what Schudson called "a journalism of anecdote," a point also made by John Nockleby, a leading torts scholar, and his colleague Shannon Curreri, who argued that journalism fails to "capture the real debate going on over the reach of the civil justice system."[13]

The million-dollar awards, wrote Nancy Marder, a professor of law at Chicago-Kent Law School, "might make good reading, but they do not describe the typical award in a medical malpractice case." From her perspective, "it is not surprising that the press chooses to focus its headlines on the million-dollar award, but in doing so it fosters the image of the runaway jury, even when there is no support that juries have gone awry in their damage awards."[14]

Marder warned that the "popular account,"[15] where juries award verdicts in the millions, should not be accepted at face value. First, there are very few civil jury trials each year in this country. Most lawsuits are resolved by motion, settlement, or alternative dispute resolution. The press, Marder explained, does not focus on "everyday events."[16] Since most awards are modest—and if they are not modest to begin with they are typically reduced by the judge—these "humdrum" events are unlikely to receive attention by the press.

In examining a small slice of total coverage—jury awards in tort actions—these scholars hand up serious indictments of how the press misrepresents the world. By its nature, the news targets the unusual: when a man bites a dog, *not* when a dog bites a man. This premise is too often left unexamined.

★ ★ ★

In the vast majority of assignments, reporters present themselves straightforwardly. Occasionally, though, reporters mask their identities. And here again, particularly in hidden-camera investigations, the focus on the aberrational shows how journalism can distort reality—even though a hidden camera is supposed to portray an undisturbed reality. The case of the Food Lion supermarket chain presents a vivid example of the legal—and journalistic—issues arising from hidden-camera reporting.

In 1992, the ABC program *Primetime Live* broadcast a report concluding that Food Lion sold unsanitary products. The report included videotapes that had been surreptitiously made by employees of ABC who had obtained jobs with the chain. Food Lion sued for fraud because the employees had lied about their background when they applied for jobs. Initially, in 1997, a federal court in Greensboro, North Carolina, awarded the Food Lion chain $5.5 million in punitive damages after finding that ABC television had committed fraud, trespass, and breach of loyalty when researching conditions in the meat-handling departments in three Food Lion supermarkets. On appeal, the verdict was modified, leaving Food Lion with a mere $2 in damages.

The truth or falsity of the *Primetime Live* broadcast was not an issue in the trial. The presiding judge, in fact, told the jurors they had to assume the broadcast was accurate. The case centered on ABC's tactics. Two female network producers secured entry-level jobs, concealing their ABC affiliation and their true purpose, which was to observe the stores' meat-handling operations. While at work they hid tiny cameras in their wigs and microphones in their bras.

"There is a pivotal question," commented Bob Steele, ethicist at the Poynter Institute in St. Petersburg, Florida. "Is it ever justifiable for a journalist to violate the principle of honesty to honor the principle upon which journalism is founded, a duty to provide the public with meaningful, accurate and comprehensive information about significant issues?"[17] His answer was a qualified "yes."

Hidden cameras, and any form of deception, he said, "should be used judiciously and rarely. They should be reserved for those exceptional stories of great public interest involving great harm to individuals or system failure at the highest levels. Furthermore, deception and hidden cameras should be used only as a reporting tool of last resort, after all other approaches to obtaining the same vital information have been exhausted or appropriately ruled out. And news organizations that choose to use deception and hidden cameras have an obligation to assure their work meets the highest professional standards."[18]

Steele's position is measured and reasonable. Richard A. Epstein, a law professor at the University of Chicago, offered a different interpretation of the Food Lion case, one that goes to the very essence of journalism as truth-telling. The undercover hidden-camera reporter, he wrote, "enters multiple premises under false pretenses, but the only information he will publish is that known to be harmful to the plaintiff. That information, moreover, will be published in a form calculated to score a knock-out blow. Any story that vindicates the plaintiff's practices ends up on the cutting room floor."[19] Epstein concluded that the "current literalist view of truth" allowed an investigative reporter to make a claim for a "literal but consciously non-representative truth." He cited the Food Lion report as an example of a story where segments of footage "were not shown in any way to be representative" of the practices of the business as a whole, thereby undermining the "entire social justification for the expose—to allow better-informed consumers to make more intelligent decisions."[20]

What Epstein underscored in the conduct of hidden-camera investigations—the "non-representative" nature of journalism—had been alluded to earlier by mid-century critics of the craft. In the late 1940s, the Hutchins Commission, which examined press practices and was named after its chair, University of Chicago president Robert Maynard Hutchins, concluded that the press "emphasizes the exceptional rather than the representative, the sensational rather than the significant." The press, the report said, "is preoccupied with these incidents to such an extent that the citizen is not supplied the information and discussion he needs to discharge his responsibilities to the community."[21] A decade later, Thomas Griffith, one of the keenest observers of journalistic practice in his day, explained the need for novelty: "Newspapermen like variety in their assignments, which is another way of saying that they may be deficient in concentration. They pursue a subject only about as far as, and rarely much further than, the passing public interest. They are servants to a fickle public; they must seize its attention by novelty, hold it by new injections of interest, and then move on to something else. A newspaper can risk boring its public at its own peril."[22]

In the words of Max Frankel, the former *New York Times* editor and a profound thinker about journalism: "In most newsrooms, the nature of news, like language itself, is taken for granted." In ranking the day's events, journalists will decide on the best story of the day. "Asked why, they'll tell you a yarn is good 'if it's important or interesting or, better yet, both.' Pressed to define important, they'll say it's news that's likely to have a psychic or material effect on world affairs, American society or local life."[23]

There is little methodology for defining news or for using sources. Journalists have few tools in their arsenals for uncovering the truth. They are not prosecutors or law-enforcement officials, and unlike law-enforcement officials, they cannot compel people to talk to them or, presumably, to tell the truth. Any conversation with a journalist obviously is voluntary, not compulsory. Journalists cannot offer the inducement of immunity or the penalty of prison to those who are reluctant or unwilling to speak. And they cannot threaten with perjury people who tell stories that do not ring true. Nor can they obtain documents by subpoena.

In the general scheme of things, the hidden cameras that Richard Epstein so objected to are not often used, and when they are, it is typically by television reporters. I had the impression that, after several stinging defeats in courts, the networks had lessened their use of hidden cameras. Then, in the fall of 2006, as I was preparing this chapter, I happened to tune into the *Today Show* on NBC. Within twenty minutes, two segments employing hidden cameras were shown. One segment promoted a *Dateline* special that was to be shown that night in the "To Catch a Predator" series. It involved the use of a hidden camera in an undercover house (fitted out with a hot tub) to record the reactions of a group of men who thought they were going to have sex with underage girls. These men, by prearrangement with authorities, were arrested on the scene. In the second segment, the reporter took a car with an easily fixed air-conditioning problem to various car repair shops. Some car repair shops were honest. Others were not.[24]

Most print outlets no longer practice undercover journalism. "There may be a once-in-a lifetime story in which the need to expose wrongdoing is so great and the means at our disposal so limited that we would misrepresent ourselves," said John Carroll, then editor of the *Baltimore Sun*. "But under almost any circumstance I could imagine we wouldn't do it."[25] What might work for television is shunned by print journalists. There are reasons for this—television has an insatiable appetite for the visual, for news unfolding before the audience's eyes.

★ ★ ★

Compared to practitioners of the traditional disciplines, journalists do not appear very systematic in the way they gather information. They do not often use the tools of social scientists. Stories are not usually enriched with data to inform the discussion. Social phenomena are not methodically examined. In explaining someone's motivation, journalists, unlike behavioral scientists, are not equipped to probe into the psychology of individuals. Increasingly, social scientists think of evidence, or of data, as quantitative; that is, as something that can be counted and then verified.[26] Journalists are only slowly beginning to use quantitative techniques, which Philip Meyer, a pioneer in this field, called "precision journalism."[27]

Nor can journalists reasonably be expected to act like scientists do. Journalists do not perform experiments like physicists. They do not work in laboratories and cannot control their conditions. The notion of repeatability has only indirect applicability to journalism. They do not rely on models like climate scientists. They do not have special tools, like astronomers, to observe their subjects. In their aversion to using mathematics, they are closer to botanists than they are to geneticists. Though there may be no unitary scientific method, the sciences of experiment and observation have one crucial common feature: they aim to see recurring features. For journalists, a trend might consist of linking up three isolated anecdotes.

In 1975, Edward Jay Epstein, a lucid and contrarian thinker, collected a series of his essays in a book titled *Between Fact and Fiction: The Problem of Journalism*. The essays were variations on the theme of how to approach truth in journalism. Epstein told how he inhabited the "antipodal" worlds of political science and journalism.[28] The discipline of political science, similar to other social sciences, he said, demands "a focus on the typical and routine elements of political behavior, and an explanation based on policies, process and institutions which presumably underlay personal deeds." Journalists, in contrast, dwell "on the atypical and extraordinary events, and [seek] explanation in personalities and anecdotes." For Epstein, journalists are caught in an inescapable bind: "They are rarely, if ever, in a position to establish the truth about an issue for themselves."[29] For Epstein, gathering news is something very different from establishing truth.

Like many contemporary observers and critics of the press, Epstein is indebted to Walter Lippmann, the journalist, thinker, and confidant of presidents, who described the inherent limitations of the press in two books, the first, at fifteen thousand words, really an extended essay, *Liberty and the News* (1920), and the other a far better known volume, *Public Opinion* (1922). "The function of news," Lippmann wrote in *Public Opinion,* "is to signalize an event; the function of truth is to bring to light hidden facts, to set them into relation with each other, and make a picture of reality on which men can act."[30] The press could draw attention to an event, but it could not itself provide the truth. In probably his most famous metaphor, Lippmann compared the press to a "beam of a searchlight that moves relentlessly about, bringing one episode and then another out of darkness into vision."[31]

Lippmann postulated that "news" could be expected to coincide with truth in only a few limited areas, such as the scores of baseball games or stock market quotes. In a modern homage to Lippmann, intended or not, the author Gay Talese, who began his career as a sportswriter, explained on the occasion of the publication of his memoir *A Writers' Life* why writers are so attracted to covering sports: "You can actually see the performing athlete. If you are a war correspondent or covering Washington or covering some country through the capital city, you are told what the news is or given some spin on what happened. But not so in the world of sports. You are ringside if you are at a fight. Or you are in the press box at a baseball game, and after the game, you can go in the locker room and talk to the person who only an hour or two before you saw in action. So you have a sense of immediacy."

He then discussed the truths of sports: "There is so much lying to the press and so much frustration on the part of the press in verifying the truth in political reporting and war reporting. So I often turn to the sports page first. It's the only part of the paper you can believe. It's the one truth section of the daily press. . . . I think it's the most honest section of a newspaper or in the periodicals."[32]

This divergence between news and truth stems not from the inadequacies of journalists, according to Lippmann, but from the constraints of the news business that limit the time, space, and resources that can be allocated to any single story. Journalism, he wrote in *Liberty and the News,* was being practiced by "untrained accidental witnesses."[33] Truth, Lippmann felt, developed out of disinterested scientific inquiry. He wanted journalists to be more objective—in the sense of emulating science by developing a sense of "evidence" and forthrightly acknowledging the limits of available information, "ascribing no more credibility to a statement than it warrants."[34] Once you go beyond what is on record at the county clerk's office, Lippmann wrote in *Public Opinion,* "all fixed standards disappear."[35]

While Lippmann was promoting greater objectivity for journalism, intellectuals and artists were moving away from objectivity. Sigmund Freud was developing his theories of the unconscious, painters were experimenting with cubism, and "the certainty of Enlightenment and Victorian views of scientifically verifiable facts gave way to the relativity of Einstein and quantum physics," wrote Jane Singer, in a shrewd analysis of how bloggers have challenged journalistic norms.[36] Lippmann's timing was off.

Charles Beard, the great twentieth-century historian, questioned objectivity in a famous speech before the American Historical Association in 1933. "Has it not been said for a century or more that each historian who writes history is a product of his age, and that his work reflects the spirit of the times, of a nation, race, group, class or section?" Beard asked. "Every student of history knows that his colleagues have been influenced in their selection and ordering of materials by their biases, prejudices, beliefs, affections, general upbringing, and experience." It is not possible, he continued, "to describe the past as it actually was, somewhat as the engineer describes a single machine." Truths of nature, ran the theory that Beard then challenged, "are to be discovered by maintaining the most severe objectivity."[37]

As much as he may have flirted with the doctrine of relativism, Beard ultimately concluded that certain criteria were fixed and that there was a place for objectivity. For Beard, the effective historian was in the position of "a statesman dealing with public affairs." His faith was "at bottom a conviction that something true can be known about the movement of history and his conviction is a subjective decision, not a purely objective discovery."[38]

So, as the intellectual world was moving away from the notion of truth as something that is verifiable, Singer wrote, "journalists were busily reaffirming and eventually codifying that notion." In the first decade of the twentieth century, Walter Williams, the founding dean of the School of Journalism at the University of Missouri, the first journalism school in this country, wrote this nation's first widely cited code of press ethics. In the "Journalist's Creed," Singer noted, Williams declared that a "journalist should 'write only what he holds in his heart to be true' and to do so based on the fundamentals of 'clear thinking and clear statement, accuracy, and fairness.'"[39] The newly formed American Society of Newspaper Editors developed its Canons of Journalism, affirming a commitment to truth and accuracy. Later, the Society of Professional Journalists developed its own ethics code, stating in the first sentence that members of the organization believed that "the duty of journalists is to serve the truth." It seemed as if the age of objectivity was ending just as journalists were taking serious note of it.

The best approach, according to Lippmann, was for journalists to acquire more of "the scientific spirit." By that he meant detachment, something different from the scientific method. The best scientific thinking today suggests that there is no single scientific method. In an essay on climate control, Naomi Oreskes, who teaches in the Department of History of Science Studies at the University of California at San Diego, argued that no method "guarantees valid conclusions that will stand up to all future scrutiny."[40] What is common to the various scientific methods is a detachment—a readiness to be open to possibilities, the very kind of detachment and readiness that characterize first-tier journalists.

In her essay, Oreskes discussed "consilience of evidence," an older approach that has come back into fashion lately. The notion of consilience, or "coming together," is generally credited to William Whewell, a nineteenth-century English philosopher, scientist, theologian, and historian of science, who said that consilience occurs when one class of facts supports the conclusion induced from a second class of facts.[41]

That notion could provide a useful way for journalists to think about evidence without resorting to a strict scientific method. The idea is not so different from what happens in a legal case. To prove a defendant guilty beyond a reasonable doubt, a prosecutor must present a variety of evidence that supports a consistent narrative of events. To sow reasonable doubt in the minds of the jurors, however, the defense may only need to show that one element of the narrative is in conflict with another. Scientists, too, look for independent lines of evidence that point to the same conclusion.

★ ★ ★

More than any other discipline, history, a soft science on the scale of disciplines, may have the most lessons to offer journalism. The central methodological problem for historians, according to Robin Winks of Yale, is to know how to interrogate witnesses, how to test evidence, how to assess the reliability and relevance of testimony.[42] This resembles very closely what journalists are supposed to do. While much of science deals with regularity in the course of events, the historian, like the journalist, deals with unique events that are not ordinarily repeated. Historians also seek out patterns, and journalists do not do enough of this.

Like other disciplines, history has experienced fundamental changes over the past 150 years. A new approach to studying history that emerged in the nineteenth century was, according to William Roger Louis, a professor of English History at the University of Texas, "that history might be perfected as a science whereby events would be recorded not only as they actually happened but in a true and universal account."[43] That approach lost its vitality, however, even as historians tried to promote the detached and objective examination of documentary evidence in order to obtain irrefutable truths about the past.[44]

Historians do not talk much about objectivity anymore—unless it is mentioned in a disapproving way. In an essay that appeared the first day of 2007 shortly berfore he died, Arthur M. Schlesinger, Jr., wrote that "all historians are prisoners of their own experience. We bring to history the preconceptions of our personalities and of our age. We cannot seize on ultimate and absolute truths. So the historian is committed to a doomed enterprise—the quest for an unattainable objectivity."[45]

In recent times, proponents of cultural anthropology, linguistical analysis, and literary criticism have explored the relevance of these disciplinary techniques to history. In a world suffused with postmodernism, wrote Mark Gilderhus, a historian at Texas Christian University, "history no longer sets forth common stories that presumably speak for the identity and experience of all readers. For many consumers of history, the narratives centering on the activities of white male elites no longer provide satisfaction, stimulation or a means to truth. We no longer possess a past commonly agreed upon. Indeed, to the contrary, we have a multiplicity of versions competing for attention and emphasizing alternatively elites and non-elites, men and women, whites and persons of color, and no good way of reconciling all the differences."[46]

Historians do not observe the events they write about, so inevitably they may differ about what really happened during a given event. Wars, after all, are not produced under laboratory conditions. Nor, as Gilderhus noted, are they observed in the sense that natural scientists make observations.[47] In reconstructing events, historians—no matter their ideology—rely on written documents. "No printed statement is without its interest," Robin Winks wrote in *The Historian as Detective.* "For historians, the destruction of old cookbooks, gazetteers, road maps, Sears Roebuck catalogues, children's books, railway timetables, or drafts of printed manuscripts, is the loss of potential evidence."[48]

In a seminal mid-twentieth-century volume, *The Idea of History,* Robin G. Collingwood, professor of metaphysical philosophy at Oxford, offered his own view of what history should be. He admonished that "a given statement, made by a given author, must never be accepted for historical truth until the credibility of the author in general and of this statement in particular has been systematically inquired into."[49] Collingwood pushed for a rigorous scrutiny of sources. "The man who makes the statement came henceforth to be regarded not as someone whose word must be taken for the truth of what he says," Collingwood wrote, "but as someone who has voluntarily placed himself in the witness-box for cross-examination."

He urged historians to abandon "scissors and paste history," where the historian's attitude toward authorities is one of "respectful attentiveness."[50] This is history constructed "by excerpting and combining the testimonies of different authorities," and it sounds a lot like the way much of contemporary journalism is practiced. Winks took history beyond its "scissors and paste" stage, saying that it is not enough for the historian merely to set one testimony against another and apply "a rigorous set of rules by which he roots out the contradictions between the witnesses." The good historian is an interrogator, Winks contended, who "wishes to know what fact may lie behind an untruth rather than merely to prove the statement to be untrue."[51]

Seeking to uncover the facts that lie behind untruths is not something that journalists ordinarily do. They practice a variation of Collingwood's "scissors and paste" history. How journalists choose their authorities can be arbitrary and often silly. Journalists are careful to provide credentials and qualifications, but far too often they rely on the "usual suspects," those who have been quoted before, those who are available on deadline, those who give pithy, digestible sound bites, and those, in the case of television, who are comfortable before the camera. It helps if the expert has written a recent book or article (as likely as not, unread by the reporter). It is certainly fine if dueling experts opine in diametrically opposite ways, thus providing balance—or at least the appearance of balance—and possibly even obscuring the issue.

Over the years, I have been called on as an authority. (It happened more often when I had the title of "dean.") One particularly absurd example of the casual use of experts occurred as I was sitting at home on a Saturday night in the midsummer of 2006, having dinner with my family. A correspondent from the local ABC station called, desperately needing my wisdom. The local television reporter, who was given my name by someone else, had no idea who I was or what I would say. But I answered my phone, and she wanted a comment.

A grand jury had issued a subpoena for a video taken by Joshua Wolf, a self-described anarchist and activist who had filmed a turbulent political protest in an area where a police car had been trashed. Some of his footage had been shown on local television, but now a grand jury demanded the outtakes. On principle, Wolf refused to surrender the video. The television reporter who called me did not want my opinion on that very important subject, but on something else. Judith Miller was visiting the Bay Area and on short notice on that Saturday, decided to drop in on Wolf in prison to show her solidarity. Miller, the former *New York Times* reporter, had spent eighty-five days in prison herself in 2005 for refusing to identify a source. She was denied access to Wolf. What, the reporter asked, did I think of *that*? I had no idea what to think and gave the frustrated reporter yet another name.

A sobering account of the problem with experts appears in a book by Philip E. Tetlock, *Expert Political Judgment, How Good Is It? How Can We Know?* Tetlock, a psychologist who teaches at the University of California at Berkeley, conducted a study demonstrating that expert political forecasts are frequently wrong. The more famous the experts were and the more they were quoted, the less reliable their predictions were likely to be. In other words, Tetlock found that people who make a business out of making predictions are no more prescient than the rest of us. In a flattering review of Tetlock's book, Louis Menand, in the *New Yorker,* elaborated on Tetlock's thesis: "People who follow current events by reading the papers and newsmagazines regularly can guess what is likely to happen about as accurately as the specialists whom the papers quote. Our system of expertise is completely inside out: it rewards bad judgments over good ones."[52]

Long before Tetlock conducted his scholarly study, Christopher Cerf and Victor Navasky in 1984 published an irreverent look at expertise, *The Experts Speak: The Definitive Compendium of Authoritative Misinformation.* For them, television is largely responsible for the deification of experts. But this deification is hollow, for television-age experts tend to be wrong as often as they are right. Television, they wrote, "is a medium where a person who is wrong at least half the time is interviewed by another person whose chief qualification is that he has no opinion on the subject. From this encounter the truth is supposed to emerge."[53]

In most instances reporters are pleased to have gotten an expert or a presumed expert to talk at all. They seemingly care more about securing an expert than they do about what the expert has to say. More sophisticated reporters, although they may not admit it, often look for someone who agrees with them, who is ideologically compatible and will spout back to them what they themselves really believe but cannot write on their own authority. Some reporters feel that they are effectively absolved from taking responsibility for the expert's opinion. "I got it totally wrong," Judith Miller confessed about her reporting during the run-up to the Iraq War, in which she uncritically accepted the Bush administration's contention that Saddam Hussein had stockpiled weapons of mass destruction. As she put it: "If your sources are wrong, you are wrong."[54]

How can this problem be cured? Tetlock suggested that using "performance feedback results" could put an end to "the old regime of close-to-zero accountability for one's pronouncements."[55] Journalists, or, for that matter, consumers, could establish a believability index for experts akin to, but more serious than, the practice adopted by many magazines in the 1990s in which they ranked various pundits on television according to how often their predictions were borne out. Albert Camus had the same urge to evaluate the purveyors of news during World War II in Paris, as mentioned earlier.

In court proceedings, experts must be qualified by "knowledge, skill, experience, training or education."[56] A third party, in this instance the judge, must agree that the expert would actually aid the jury's understanding of the issue. Otherwise, the expert is not permitted to testify. Journalism would be immeasurably improved if, in the spirit of the rules of evidence, journalists tightened up their choice of experts and quoted only those who were truly qualified to say something worthy.

THREE

LOOKING AT THE LAW

Hearsay is secondhand information. It occurs when witnesses testify not about something they personally saw or heard, but about something someone else told them that they saw or said. At trial, hearsay is generally inadmissible, but over the years exceptions to this rule have been carved out. Generally, though, hearsay is not the best evidence. The original account is not delivered under oath. The jury cannot assess the demeanor of the person from whom the knowledge springs. And, most importantly, the truthfulness of the person whose words are spoken cannot be tested by cross-examination. In other words, the other side in an adversary proceeding would not have the opportunity to confront and cross-examine the witness who originally saw or heard something. In a legal proceeding, it is crucial to understand the purpose for which the evidence is being offered. Is the statement being offered to prove the truth of the matter it asserts, or just to prove that the statement was made?[1]

Journalists rely heavily on the equivalent of hearsay. They are not bound by the rules of evidence, of course, but the overuse of hearsay deprives readers of the tools to question statements. Readers often do not know who the ultimate source of a statement is or how the journalist came to know what was reported. The hearsay rule—really a set of rules, because of its many exceptions formulated over time—is just one legal concept that can shed light on the journalistic enterprise and its pursuit of journalistic truth.

The origins of the hearsay rule are generally traced to the 1603 trial of Sir Walter Raleigh, a man of action (a soldier, sailor, explorer, and adventurer) and a man of letters (a poet and historian). Much earlier, Sir Walter Raleigh had been a court favorite. One story has him winning the favor of Queen Elizabeth I by laying down his opulent cloak in the mud to protect the queen's slippers. With her death, he quickly slipped out of favor with her successor, King James, son of Mary Queen of Scots. Suspected of being a spy for Spain, Raleigh was brought to trial on conspiracy charges in late 1603. He was accused of plotting with Lord Cobham to advance the king's cousin, Arabella Stuart, to the throne. The primary witness against Raleigh was Lord Cobham, a presumed friend. The trial ended with a verdict pronouncing Raleigh guilty of high treason on the basis of testimony of evidence not introduced directly in court. As traditionally understood, the rule limiting hearsay testimony was designed to prevent the kind of abuse that permitted the conviction of Raleigh on an unsworn out-of-court statement by Raleigh's alleged accomplice, Lord Cobham, who betrayed him, at least temporarily.

Lord Cobham had implicated Raleigh in the plot in an examination before the Privy Council as well as in a letter. At Raleigh's trial in Winchester (a plague was raging in London, so the court moved south), documents implicating Raleigh were read to the jury, but Raleigh argued that Cobham had lied to save himself: "Cobham is absolutely in the King's mercy; to excuse me cannot avail him; by accusing me he may hope for favor." Suspecting that Cobham would recant, Raleigh demanded that Cobham be present at the trial so that he could confront and cross-examine him, arguing that "the Proof of the Common Law is by witness and jury: let Cobham be here, let him speak it. Call my accuser before my face." The judges refused, and, despite Raleigh's protestations that he was being tried "by the Spanish Inquisition," the jury convicted him. Raleigh was sentenced to be hanged, drawn, and quartered.[2]

But Raleigh was neither hanged, nor drawn, nor quartered. Instead, he was pardoned, on the condition that he would be imprisoned in the Tower of London. He spent a dozen years there before being released and sent on a mining expedition to South America. The expedition failed, and upon his return to London, in 1618, Raleigh was seized and summarily beheaded, apparently to appease the anger of Spain.

Outrage at the injustice done to Raleigh helped lead to the introduction of the hearsay rule and the constitutional right of confrontation. By the end of the seventeenth century, the rule against hearsay was widely recognized. Raleigh's demands to face his accuser were cited at length more than four hundred years later by U.S. Supreme Court Justice Antonin Scalia as one of the precedents for the right to confront one's accusers.[3] (A rough journalistic analogy would be the odious practice of anonymously quoting someone who said something pejoratively. "'Tom just was not up to playing tackle for the Giants,' a colleague who requested anonymity said." How can Tom rebut that?)

The contemporary case, *Crawford v. Washington,* was not politically charged like Raleigh's. Rather, it was a run-of-the-mill assault prosecution in which the U.S. Supreme Court struck down the conviction of a Washington state man because the original jury had heard a taped statement made by the defendant's wife, who had not been allowed to testify at trial. In 2004, the Court ruled that the jury should not have heard the statement because the defendant could not question his wife about what she had said. In this case, Michael Crawford had stabbed Kenneth Lee, ostensibly during an argument over whether Lee had sexually assaulted

Crawford's wife, Sylvia. Police interviewed both Michael and Sylvia Crawford. During the first interview, the couple seemed to corroborate each other's story. But when interviewed separately a second time, Sylvia's account contradicted her husband's on whether he had acted in self-defense in stabbing Lee.

Crawford was charged with assault and attempted murder. He invoked Washington state's marital privilege, thereby preventing his wife from testifying at his trial. Still, the prosecution was able to get the tape-recorded second interview into evidence under an exception to the marital privilege. Crawford was convicted of assault while armed with a deadly weapon. On appeal, Justice Scalia, writing for a 7–2 court, held that Sylvia's statement had not been properly admitted into evidence. He announced a new confrontation clause rule consistent with the framers' understanding: "Testimonial statements of witnesses absent from trial have been admitted only where the declarant is unavailable, and only where the defendant has had a prior opportunity to cross-examine."[4]

Legal rules for admitting evidence set a high bar—a bar that, if applied to journalism, would make life unbearably difficult for journalists. Reporters would likely find it impossible to present evidence at all within the time constraints they face. It would be foolhardy to suggest that journalists play by the legal rules. What they find out is not meant to stand up in court. A reporter may be absolutely convinced that a story is correct. The sources are impeccable. The facts have been checked. The facts may not be provable in court, but the reporter is not writing for a court. Nevertheless, understanding legal rules, such as hearsay, its history, and its many exceptions, can help journalists evaluate the evidence they obtain in a clearer, more strategic way.

The rule against hearsay was described by John Henry Wigmore, the great early twentieth-century authority on evidence, as "that most characteristic rule of the Anglo-American law of evidence—a rule which may be esteemed, next to jury trial, the greatest contribution of that eminently practical legal system to the world's methods of procedure."[5] The danger of admitting hearsay is that it would take away the other side's opportunity to confront and cross-examine the witness who originally saw or heard something. But, in a real sense, the rule against hearsay can also cut against truth-telling. The rule is just one of the procedural rules showing that the adversarial system, so honored in our country, is not necessarily concerned with the truth of *all* underlying facts, but instead with the truth of facts presented against an accused. Indeed, lawyers can present a highly selective version of truth.

The origins of the adversarial system can be traced back to primitive systems of trial by combat. It is a system based on the theory that the best way to attain justice is to have two lawyers fight it out, obeying a set of well-established procedures. A lawyer is obligated to present the evidence in a way that puts his or her client in the best light. To even the playing field, lawyers, under rules of discovery, must assist one another in their search for material. But the defense lawyer has no duty to present evidence that would harm a client. In a criminal trial, for instance, the challenge for defense lawyers is to persuade the jury that prosecution witnesses should not be believed. They do that through cross-examination, which Wigmore called "the greatest legal engine ever invented for the discovery of truth."[6]

The adversarial system presupposes, in the words of Michael Asimow, who teaches at the law school at the University of California at Los Angeles, at least a rough equality between the two sides in "their advocacy skills, their experience, and in the sources they bring to the struggle."[7] Therefore, Asimow argued, "a trial lawyer's responsibility under the adversary model is not to assist and facilitate the jury's search for truth, but, whenever possible within the rules, to obstruct and obfuscate that search if such favors the interests of the client." The reality of legal practice is that often the more skillful lawyer, not the most virtuous case, wins the day. The work of lawyers, Asimow contended, "has little to do with securing justice or in revealing truth and everything to do with using craft to serve the interests of clients."[8] To make his point, Asimow quoted from the 1998 movie *A Civil Action,* in which defense lawyer Jerome Facher (Robert Duvall) said to the plaintiff's lawyer, Jan Schlictmann (John Travolta), as they sat in the hallway awaiting the verdict: "If you're really looking for the truth, Jan, look for it where it is. At the bottom of a bottomless pit."[9]

The hearsay rule is designed to exclude evidence that cannot be tested for reliability because there is no cross-examination. Sometimes evidence that may be relevant to a trial is not admissible for other reasons—for example, because it runs afoul of other policy considerations or because it is excessively prejudicial. For instance, under the exclusionary rule, evidence that is obtained illegally cannot be admitted in court as it violates the Fourth Amendment of the U.S. Constitution, which protects citizens against unreasonable searches and seizures. The exclusionary rule, as the late Justice Potter Stewart observed in an interview after he left the bench, is not meant "to grant certain guilty defendants a windfall by letting them go free—though it sometimes does do that." The objective is rather to protect all citizens, particularly the innocent, against police searches based on personal malice, incompetence, or political motivation.[10] In the memorable formulation of the great judge Benjamin Cardozo, the rationale of the rule is that "the criminal is to go free because the constable has blundered."[11] In other words, the rule is designed to penalize police and deter police misconduct.

The doctrine of "the fruit of the poisonous tree" is an extension of the exclusionary rule, and its rationale is also to stop police from using illegal means to obtain evidence. If the source of the evidence—"the tree"—is poisoned, so too are the results—"the fruit,"—of that evidence. Thus, for example, a suspect's admission to the police of committing a crime is not admissible at trial if the suspect was not read his or her *Miranda* warnings.[12] That is, suspects must be clearly informed that they have the right to remain silent and that anything they say may be used against them in court, and they also must be clearly informed that they have the right to consult with a lawyer and to have that lawyer present during an interrogation. If, say, the suspect tells the police the location of the stolen gun, that admission cannot be introduced as evidence at a trial if no *Miranda* warnings were given. Neither can the gun. Or if a policeman conducts an unconstitutional search of a witness and examines the suspect's computer, which reveals the address of a witness, that witness cannot testify. The testimony would be a poisoned fruit of the illegal search.

Another long-standing rule, the statute of limitations, limits the time in which a case can be brought. Federal Judge Jack Weinstein, who sits in the Eastern District of New York and once taught evidence at Columbia Law School, issued a stunning decision in June 2006 to dismiss the guilty verdicts of two retired New York City detectives who were the centerpieces of the so-called Mafia cops corruption case, in which the detectives were charged with carrying out contract murders for a Mafia crime family. In reviewing the evidence presented at trial, Weinstein concluded that it "overwhelmingly established the defendants' participation in a large number of heinous and violent crimes,"[13] including conspiracy and eight gangland murders, all in Brooklyn in the 1980s and 1990s. Nevertheless, Judge Weinstein reversed the convictions of the two detectives, Louis J. Eppolito and Stephen Caracappa, because the five-year statute of limitations in their case had effectively run out.

It did not matter that earlier in 2006, they had been convicted of some of the most brazen corruption charges in recent memory. It did not matter that a jury found that Eppolito and Caracappa had participated, as paid assassins, in killings for the mob. The judge said that he had no choice but to let them go because the statute of limitations in conspiracy cases had run out. "It will undoubtedly appear peculiar to many people that heinous criminals such as the defendants, having been found guilty on overwhelming evidence of the most despicable crimes of violence, should go unwhipped of justice," Weinstein wrote. "Yet our Constitution, statutes and morality require that we be ruled by the law, not vindictiveness or advantages of the moment."[14]

* * *

Rules governing legal evidence are designed to get at the truth by excluding unreliable information, such as hearsay, from consideration. But these rules also guarantee that the legal process only reaches a partial truth. Otherwise valuable evidence is excluded because our courts place a high value on stopping police misbehavior and assuring timely trials. Similarly, legal privileges, such as those that exist in the attorney-client or doctor-patient relationship, exclude reliable information in order to advance a competing social policy. "Because this is a high price to pay, the social policy furthered by a privilege must be quite weighty to justify the cost to the truth-finding function of the legal process," wrote Geoffrey R. Stone, who teaches constitutional law and evidence at the University of Chicago Law School. The most entrenched of the privileges is the one that protects confidential communications between a lawyer and a client regarding legal advice. The rationale of this privilege, wrote Stone, is that "clients will not be candid with their attorneys if everything clients disclose to their attorneys can be used against them in court, and attorneys cannot give sound legal advice to their clients if clients are less than candid in their disclosures to their attorneys."[15]

These privileges and procedural rules should give journalists much to think about on two levels. On one level, journalists must recognize the built-in limitations of the legal system in arriving at truth. On a second level, journalists might well consider adopting, at least informally, variations of these legal rules. For instance, should information obtained by journalistic subterfuge ever be discarded? Do journalists have a duty to read subjects the equivalent of *Miranda* warnings so as to let them know the potential drawbacks of cooperating? Should an informal journalistic statute of limitations stop journalists from looking at youthful indiscretions of public officials? In a hearsay context, should journalists ever report something that is so far removed from their experience that they do not even know the ultimate source of the information?

Journalists rely broadly on the counterpart to hearsay, probably much more than they should. But the hearsay rule has many formally recognized exceptions, and journalists in their reporting can be guided by these exceptions. Although in a legal setting hearsay is surely not the best type of evidence, its unreliability may sometimes be overstated. Indeed, courts are constantly admitting hearsay evidence under the numerous exceptions to the rule. That means that in many instances judges and juries are allowed to hear out-of-court statements without the litigant or defendant having an opportunity to cross-examine the person who made the statement. For instance, the "dying declaration" exception rests on the traditional belief that persons on their deathbed will be truthful. Similarly, the law recognizes spontaneous or "excited utterances" as signs of truth-telling. The law suggests that people in a state of high stress have little time to lie. The *res gestae* exception rests on the notion that some words and some deeds may be inextricably linked. For instance, pornography confiscated from a child molester might be taken to suggest that the victims were shown pornography. Also, a statement a person makes despite knowing he or she may face criminal charges as a result of the statement is admissible. Finally, under the "business and public records" exception, the law assumes that regularly kept records typically have a high degree of accuracy. Once authenticated under the business records exception, whole categories of records can be admitted, including school records, medical records, and financial records.[16]

The similarities in journalism to hearsay exceptions are plentiful. Journalists tend to confer greater trust to a statement a person makes against his or her own best interests than to a statement that may be self-serving. When interviewing a source, journalists routinely feel that the original responses are more truthful than ones made after the source has a chance to reconsider, and therefore, most journalists refuse to let interview subjects edit their comments at a later time. Whether it would be excluded under the hearsay rule or admitted under a hearsay exception, a good deal of the information reporters gather is secondhand information. As Walter Lippmann noted in *Public Opinion,* "in all but exceptional cases, journalism is not a first hand report of the raw material."[17] In an anecdote involving Babe Ruth, Lippmann pointed out that journalists are often more comfortable with official, secondhand versions of reality than they are with their own direct observations. "Not long ago Babe Ruth was jailed for speeding," Lippmann related in a footnote. "Released from jail just before the afternoon game started, he rushed into his waiting automobile, and made up for time lost in jail by breaking the speed laws on his way to the ball grounds. No policeman stopped him, but a reporter timed him, and published his speed the next morning. Babe Ruth is an exceptional man. Newspapers cannot time all motorists. They have to take their news about speeding from the police."[18]

From this, Leon V. Sigal concluded, in an astute essay entitled "Sources Make the News," that "news is not what happens, but what someone says has happened or will happen." Since reporters are seldom in a position to witness events firsthand, they are beholden to the accounts of others. Reporters minimize "explicit interpretation," Sigal wrote, "by eschewing value-laden vocabulary and by writing in the third-person impersonal, not the first-person personal. Above all, they try to attribute the story, and especially any interpretation of what it means, to sources."[19]

Judith Miller, the Pulitzer Prize–winning reporter for the *New York Times,* is a leitmotif that runs through this book. In her coverage of the period leading up to the invasion of Iraq, she wrote or cowrote a series of exclusive stories in 2002 and 2003 about how Saddam Hussein had either purchased weapons of mass destruction or was in the process of doing so. Miller relied on well-placed sources, including Ahmed Chalabi, the Iraqi exile with close ties to the Bush administration, and his patrons in the Pentagon, to whom she had special access. Unsurprisingly, she parroted the neoconservative party line. A story she wrote in the late summer of 2002 with another *Times* reporter, Michael Gordon, for instance, gave details on how Iraq had "stepped up" its quest for nuclear weapons and embarked on a worldwide hunt for materials to make an atomic bomb. The story strongly suggested that Iraq had attempted to purchase specially designed aluminum, presumably destined to be made into components to enrich uranium.

One paragraph has "Iraqi defectors who once worked for the nuclear weapons establishment" telling American officials "that acquiring nuclear arms is again a top Iraqi priority."[20]

This is murky reporting. The readers do not know who the American officials are. They do not know who the defectors are. They have no way to judge the credibility of the defectors—or of the officials, for that matter. Such sourcing, were it in a court context, would be inadmissible. A later paragraph in the article reads: "An Iraqi defector said Mr. Hussein had also heightened his efforts to develop new types of chemical weapons." But we have no idea how the defector knows this.[21]

In hindsight, we know that Judith Miller misled her audience with her reporting. In explaining what went wrong, she accepted responsibility. But her contrition rings hollow, for she said that getting it right was beyond her control. In that way, she did journalism a disservice.

Not long after the appearance of these articles and their refutation, in a confusing display of principle, Miller served eighty-five days in jail to protect a source in a national security matter—even though the source, I. Lewis Libby, later said that he needed no protection. Shortly after her release, she resigned under pressure from the *Times*. For a short time, she had occupied center stage in American journalism. During this period, she went from goat, to martyr, to outcast and became, in her words, "a lightning rod for public fury over the intelligence failures that helped lead our country to war."[22] In defending her reporting, Miller took a very narrow view in defining her job. Her job as a reporter, she said, was not "to assess the government's information and be an independent intelligence analyst" but simply to tell the paper's readers "what the government thought about Iraq's arsenal."[23]

Her stories were wrong, she repeatedly said, because her

sources were wrong. That was all there was to it. "W.M.D.—I got it totally wrong," was her explanation when she was quoted in an exceedingly thorough *New York Times* analysis of her reporting and her jailing. As noted earlier, she simultaneously accepted blame while blaming others: "The analysts, the experts and the journalists who covered them—we were all wrong. If your sources are wrong, you are wrong. I did the best job that I could."[24]

Three days later, in testimony to the U.S. Senate Committee on the Judiciary on the "urgent need" of a national shield law to protect reporters and their sources, she sounded the same theme: "As I painfully learned while covering intelligence estimates of Saddam Hussein's weapons of mass destruction, we are only as good as our sources. If they are wrong, we will be wrong."[25] She went on to testify: "Whistleblowers or those who engage in spinning reporters are not usually saints, and journalists should not demand that they be so." In elaborating, she uttered this odd non sequitur: "While reporters must try to understand why someone is telling them something, what counts far more than their motivation is the truth and significance of what they are saying."

Was Miller right in saying that as a reporter she was only as good as her sources? Was she right in separating the motivations of her sources from truth-telling? That Iraq had some weapons of mass destruction was a widely shared assumption, but not one that every journalist accepted. In the great tradition of challenging official groupthink, many journalists—both in the mainstream and in the independent press—were not fooled. Miller chose to convey the official line rather than to be appropriately skeptical of leaks that were officially sanctioned.

In a radio debate with Michael Massing, who wrote "Now They Tell Us," a powerful two-part critique of prewar coverage, Miller lectured him on being out of his depth and then described her role: "My job was not to collect information and analyze it independently as an intelligence agency. My job was to tell readers of the *New York Times* as best as I could figure out, what people inside the government who had very high security clearances, who were not supposed to talk to me, were saying to one another about what they thought Iraq had and did not have in the area of weapons of mass destruction."[26]

In a highly unusual unsigned editors' note to its readers, the *Times* confessed error in its coverage and attempted to explain how it all happened: "In most cases, what we reported was an accurate reflection of the state of our knowledge at the time, much of it painstakingly extracted from intelligence agencies that were themselves dependent on sketchy information. . . . But we have found a number of instances of coverage that was not as rigorous as it should have been. In some cases information that was controversial then, and seems questionable now, was insufficiently qualified or allowed to stand unchallenged. Looking back, we wish we had been more aggressive in re-examining the claims as new evidence emerged—or failed to emerge." The "problematic articles" shared a common feature, the editor's note said: "They depended at least in part on information from a circle of Iraqi informants, defectors and exiles bent on 'regime change' in Iraq, people whose credibility has come under increasing public debate in recent weeks."[27]

Howell Raines, the executive editor of the paper when Miller was writing her stories, defended the coverage. In the *Los Angeles Times,* and on "Romenesko," a popular website for journalists, Raines said the reporters "acted in good faith to present the best version of the facts they could obtain at the time." For him, "it is inevitable that newspaper stories of this kind—usually based on information from interested parties in government and elsewhere—are incomplete and in some cases reflect the agenda of the sources."[28]

These competing views of one editor, Bill Keller, who expressed his misgivings in the editors' note, and his predecessor are not compatible. In this context, another rule of law—the "republication rule"—can be helpful to journalists in sorting through claims that sources make. The general application of defamation law holds the republisher of a defamatory falsehood just as culpable as the original speaker. Under the common law, one who republishes a defamatory statement is liable in equal measure to the original defamer. Even in nondefamatory settings, journalists should be especially careful about repeating statements others have made.

To understand the rationale of this rule, we must separate two levels of truth that the press must deal with when it comes to government accusations. The first level is concerned with whether a news story reports the accusation itself accurately and fairly. The second and deeper level, according to two authors of a 2005 law review article on this subject, Jonathan Donnellan and Justin Peacock, "is concerned with the truth of the underlying charge itself, regardless of whether it was accurately recounted."[29]

Like the hearsay rule, the republication rule has many exceptions. If the republished statement comes directly from a public record, a public proceeding, or a public official's statements at a public event, such as a press conference, many states have adopted "fair report" privileges that protect republication. In other words, the common-law fair report privilege shields most reporting concerning official government accusations from liability. The republication doctrine, wrote Donnellan and Peacock, states that "when you republish a defamatory statement by another, you effectively own it and may be held liable just as if you made it yourself." So far as the republication doctrine is concerned, "it is irrelevant that you gave full attribution to the original speaker and quoted him accurately."[30] The rule itself is a strict one, and there is no escaping the question it presents: Does the press have a responsibility to find the deeper truth, the ultimate truth of the underlying allegations?

FOUR

TRUTH IN THE BALANCE

The lead story of the *New York Times* on Monday, August 14, 1972, described the New York State Commission of Investigation's accusation that the New York City Police Department had failed to investigate reports that seventy-two police officers had engaged in narcotics trafficking. Tucked away on this slow news day, deep on page 33, the wedding page that day, was what appeared to be a relatively benign, unimportant story: a nine-paragraph item written by Jack Devlin. The reporter was sixty-one years old and had been at the *Times* since 1949. He had been a longtime nature reporter for the paper and had generally stayed out of trouble. Devlin was a kind, gentle man whose article later became the centerpiece of path-breaking litigation in a federal trial in which scientists who were mentioned in the article claimed the *New York Times* had recklessly published an article questioning their conclusions about the effect of pesticides on the nation's bird population. On the witness stand, Devlin appeared at times to be a confused man with a failing memory. (Later in life, Devlin, with his wife, wrote the authorized biography of Roger Tory Peterson, the ornithologist who was heir to John James Audubon.)

The none-too-enticing headline of Devlin's article read: "Pesticide Spokesmen Accused of 'Lying' on Higher Bird Count." Devlin began his story this way: "Segments of the pesticide industry and certain 'scientist spokesmen' are accused in the current issue of *American Birds* of 'lying' by saying that bird life in North America is thriving despite the use of DDT."[1]

American Birds, published by the National Audubon Society, had carried an editorial preface, written by the magazine's editor, Robert Arbib, Jr., charging that "anytime you hear a 'scientist' say [that large numbers of birds are not dying as a result of DDT], you are in the presence of someone who is being paid to lie, or is parroting something he knows little about."[2] The publication did not identify the people it described as "spokesmen." Following through as a good reporter typically does, Devlin decided to do a story and asked Arbib who these spokesmen were. Arbib readily provided the names and positions of five scientists. Devlin reached three of the five and included their denials in his story. In other words, in seemingly workmanlike fashion, in conformance with the journalistic norms of his time, Devlin reported on an accusation that had appeared elsewhere, but named five scientists whom Arbib had said he'd had in mind as he wrote his editorial preface.

Unwittingly, Devlin had stumbled into a public controversy that had simmered for at least twenty-five years between proponents and opponents of the widespread use of DDT and other pesticides. On one side was the National Audubon Society, which ever since 1900 had conducted and publicized its annual Christmas Bird Count, which used teams of society members, including many amateur ornithologists, to conduct a survey of bird life throughout the nation. The Audubon Society published the tabulation annually in *American Birds,* and these statistics were considered by many authorities to be the most reliable indicator of the ebb and flow of bird populations in North America. On the other side were certain scientists questioning the effects of DDT on the bird population. They included, by 1972, J. Gordon Edwards, a professor at what was then San Jose State College, whose expertise was entomology and conservation. Edwards and the other scientists mentioned in Devlin's article placed the bird count in the context of the larger public controversy of DDT—a controversy vividly brought to public attention with the publication, in 1962, of *Silent Spring* by Rachel Carson, widely considered the mother of the modern environmental movement. The scientists took the position that the Audubon Society's Christmas count data showed that birds had *increased* in numbers despite the use of DDT and other pesticides.

Audubon officials felt that the scientists had misconstrued the data of the Christmas Bird Count and that, in fact, as Arbib pointed out, many species "high on the food chain" had suffered "serious declines" as a direct result of pesticide contamination. The scientists had claimed in previous papers that the increased use of pesticides, including DDT, was actually associated with a very rapidly increasing bird population, directly contradicting Arbib and the Audubon position, which served as the basis for the prediction of a coming extinction of birds. Audubon supporters asserted a much simpler explanation for the seeming paradox that the number of birds had increased as the use of DDT had spread: there were not more birds, but more birders. Audubon argued that the apparent increases in the numbers of birds on the Christmas Bird Count resulted from ever-increasing numbers of birders in the field, better access to the areas where the counts were made, better knowledge of where to find the birds, and increasing sophistication in the identification of birds.

How could Jack Devlin, a nonconfrontational lover of nature, be expected to referee a controversy over the effect of DDT on the growth or decline of avian populations?

The scientists sued in federal court. The jury was instructed that the *Times* could be found guilty of "actual malice" if Devlin had serious doubts about the truth of the statement that the scientists were paid liars, even if he did not have any doubt that he was reporting Arbib's allegations faithfully. The jury found the *Times* and an Audubon employee liable for defamation and awarded the plaintiffs more than $60,000. The jury interpreted the evidence before it to indicate that Devlin showed a reckless disregard for whether the accusation was true or false. The key to the jury's verdict was the finding that the reporter had made no more than a modest effort to confirm the validity of the National Audubon Society's accusations. The jury felt that the *Times* could have waited to publish the story, as it was not the kind of "hot news" that required immediate dissemination. In fact, ten days before the story was published, the *Times* learned that two of the five suspected scientists were not employed by the pesticide industry and therefore could not have been "paid liars."

On appeal, the issue became whether a libel judgment could stand against the *Times* even though the paper had published an article that accurately reported what someone else had written. In this instance, the *Times* had repeated potentially defamatory accusations by the National Audubon Society against five scientists who disagreed with environmentalists over the impact of DDT on wildlife. Like Judith Miller's reports on weapons of mass destruction in Iraq, Devlin's article was an example of republication.

The newspaper was lucky. The appeal was assigned to a panel of judges on the Manhattan-based Second Circuit Court of Appeals that included Irving Kaufman, who had been uncommonly friendly to the *Times* over the years and was a highly visible champion of a free press. In this particular case, *Edwards v. the National Audubon Society and the New York Times*,[3] Kaufman in 1977 staked out a new area of libel law and created a new First Amendment right. Single-handedly, he established a new constitutional defense to libel law—the privilege of "neutral reportage." The court ruled that when a newspaper accurately reports defamatory charges made by a responsible organization against a public figure, the publication may not be held liable for its accurate reporting. "We do not believe," the court stated, "that the press may be required under the First Amendment to suppress newsworthy statements merely because it has serious doubts regarding their truth." The First Amendment, the ruling said, protects "the accurate and disinterested reporting" of newsworthy accusations whatever "the reporter's private views of their validity."[4]

On one level, of course, this opinion was a triumph for the press, but under close examination it might not be so helpful as it appears. Ted Glasser, who teaches at Stanford, was one of the few scholars who commented on this opinion. He was particularly critical of the court's reasoning. "Objective reporting virtually precludes responsible reporting," he wrote shortly after the opinion was published, "if by responsible reporting we mean a willingness on the part of the reporter to be accountable for what is reported. Objectivity requires only that reporters be accountable for *how* they report, not *what* they report."[5]

The *Edwards* court had made this very clear: "The public interest in being fully informed," the court said, demands that the press be afforded the freedom to report newsworthy accusations "without assuming responsibility for them."[6] The court emphasized, moreover, that the charges must be made by a "responsible source": when a "responsible, prominent organization like the National Audubon Society makes serious charges against a public figure," Kaufman wrote, First Amendment protection kicks in. He added, "What is newsworthy about such accusations is that they were made."[7] In so restricting the reach of its opinion to "responsible" folks, the *Edwards* court reflects, in Glasser's words, "the unfortunate bias of objective reporting—a bias in favor of leaders and officials, the prominent and the elite."[8]

Nearly thirty years later, the decision in *Edwards* still has limited applicability. The freedom of the press to air accusations made by prominent organizations, known as the "neutral reportage" doctrine, has generated a mixed reaction in courts around the country, and the U.S. Supreme Court has chosen not to review the issue. It remains a durable doctrine, but it is particularly controversial among journalists wishing to do their jobs fairly. Recently (or recent in a judicial time frame), the California Supreme Court limited the reach of the neutral reportage privilege in that state. This occurred in a case that arose from the 1968 assassination of then presidential candidate Robert F. Kennedy.

Khalid Khawar, a freelance photographer covering Kennedy's campaign, was photographed near Kennedy a few minutes before he was assassinated. Twenty years later, in 1988, Roundtable Publishing released a book written by Robert Morrow that identified Kennedy's "true" assassin as a young Pakistani. In the book, *The Senator Must Die: The Murder of Robert Kennedy,* Morrow, a former CIA agent, presented the theory that Sirhan Sirhan was actually a decoy and that Kennedy's killers were a Pakistani named Ali Ahmand, the Mafia, and Iranian agents. Morrow included in the book a photograph of the man he said was Ahmand. The man identified as Ahmand was actually Khalid Khawar. Of the 25,000 books printed, only 350 were sold.

In April 1989, the *Globe,* a supermarket tabloid, published an article about the book and reprinted the Khawar photograph with the headline: "Former CIA Agent Claims: Iranians Killed Bobby Kennedy for the Mafia." Khawar, who by then had left the world of photography and had turned to farming, sued along with his father. They settled the lawsuit with the book's publisher before the trial, and a default judgment was entered against the author. A jury trial in 1994 entered claims against the *Globe* and awarded Khawar $1.175 million in compensatory and punitive damages.

The California Court of Appeals, the state's intermediate appellate court, affirmed that ruling in 1996 and rejected the *Globe*'s neutral reportage argument, holding that the newspaper was obliged to conduct its own investigation into allegations made by others. In fact, the *Globe* had published the story about Morrow's book without conducting even the most routine reporting. The Libel Defense Resource Center, an advocacy group on behalf of defendants in libel lawsuits, noted in its newsletter how the court interpreted the testimony of the *Globe*'s managing editor: "The court cites testimony of the managing editor that he failed to contact any of the 2,300 people who were present on the night of the assassination as evidence supporting a finding that the *Globe* was purposefully avoiding the truth."[9]

The case raised the question of whether neutral reportage should be expanded to include plaintiffs who are not well known at all and are just private figures. In 1998, *Khawar v. Globe International Inc.* reached the California Supreme Court, which unanimously affirmed that the neutral reportage privilege does not extend to accusations made against a relatively obscure individual.[10]

Even if the neutral reportage doctrine has not become the law of the land, the reasoning behind it challenges the very notions of balance and objectivity. As Ted Glasser noted in his critical essay about Judge Kaufman's opinion, the convention of objective reporting, which emerged in this country about a century ago, provided a set of routine procedures that journalists could use in the effort to make their news stories seem objective. For journalists, Glasser observed, "this means interviews with sources, and it ordinarily means official sources with impeccable credentials. It means juxtaposing conflicting truth-claims, where truth-claims are reported as 'fact' regardless of their validity."[11] Balanced coverage—that is, telling both sides of a story—became one of the pillars of traditional journalism. But truth cannot be achieved by journalists acting as stenographers, merely balancing opposing statements. They must dig beneath the rhetoric to get at the primary sources.

John Harris, then national political editor of the *Washington Post,* articulately captured the essence of this issue in a 2006 online conversation with a reader of the newspaper. Harris noted, "It is a very common criticism that journalistic conventions about objectivity and fairness require us to put truth and falsehood on an equal plane. 'Republicans praised the sunny day, but Democrats asserted it is really raining.'" For Harris, journalists "should state the facts and truth as plainly as we can report it, not take refuge behind 'he said/she said.' Is it raining, or not?" The reporter can know that directly and does not need dueling voices to make it evident. Harris admonished, however, that "it is also true that we in the press are not a 'High Court of Truth.' Many things that seem self-evidently true to partisans on one side do not look that way to others. So this gives us an obligation to present divergent points of view, and acknowledge that information is fragmentary and the 'truth' is subject to many interpretations. That is what I mean by fairness."[12]

Thus, the questioning of fairness, balance, and objectivity, initiated by academics, has spilled over to newsrooms. Whether it is called neutral reportage or not (and it is mostly not), journalists like Harris are challenging the basic notion of their craft that generations of teachers and editors have drilled into them: that when you print a controversial statement, it must be followed by a balanced response from someone on the other side. To be sure, in reporting political or legal stories it is usually appropriate to report both sides of an issue. But this need not be done in rote fashion no matter what the evidence is on either side.

There are signs now that audiences, or at least sophisticated audiences, have become impatient with certain journalistic conventions. In one of his last columns before departing in 2006 for a position at the journalism school at the University of Missouri, Jeffrey Dworkin, the ombudsman for National Public Radio, wrote: "If my e-mail box is any indication, more and more listeners are finding NPR's traditional approach to reporting both sides of an issue to be increasingly unsatisfactory and frustrating." From his position, he sensed "a rising anxiety and impatience among large numbers of NPR listeners who urge that the network take a more activist—or at least a more openly skeptical—role in the media landscape of the United States." He quoted a listener, who wrote in: "On the one hand this and on the other hand that—that is the evasion of journalistic responsibility." The listener called it "junk food for the ears." Every story, Dworkin suggested, does not have two sides.[13]

The fault lines inherent in the balanced approach to journalism were vividly exposed by former Vice President Al Gore, a one-time reporter who had a decidedly mixed relationship with reporters during his political career. Often reporters, who liked the positions he espoused, were uncomfortable with his stiffness. Within weeks after Gore lost the presidency in 2000, he made an unlikely journey to New York, where he taught a course at the Columbia Graduate School of Journalism, where I was dean. It was an awkward fit. Gore wanted press attention, but only to a point. He liked being photographed going to class, often with famous guests such as Alan Greenspan, David Letterman, or Rupert Murdoch. But Gore would not talk to reporters or let them sit in on his class. He wished to be seen by the press, but not heard, all of which caused headaches for me.

Gore's writing gifts, though, are unquestioned. Atop the paperback best-seller list for much of the summer of 2006 was Gore's *An Inconvenient Truth,* which contained stunning pictures along with dire warnings of global warming. In the book, where the text appeared in mostly large, easy-to-read type, as well as in a fulllength documentary that played at movie houses during the summer and won an Oscar, Gore juxtaposed two studies, one about global warming, the other about the press's coverage of the subject. This is what he said about the two studies:

> A University of California at San Diego scientist, Naomi Oreskes, published in *Science* magazine a massive study of every peer-reviewed science journal article on global warming in the past ten years. She and her team selected a random sample of 928 articles, representing almost ten per cent of the total, and carefully analyzed how many of the articles agreed or disagreed with the prevailing consensus view. About a quarter of the articles in the sample dealt with aspects of global warming that did not involve any discussion of the central elements of the consensus. Of the three-quarters that did address these main points, the percentage that disagreed with the consensus? Zero. . . .
>
> Well, alongside the study of peer-reviewed scientific journal articles that show 0% in disagreement with the consensus on global warming, another large study was conducted of all the articles on global warming during the previous fourteen years in the four newspapers considered by the authors of the study to be the most influential in America: the *New York Times,* the *Washington Post,* the *LA Times* and the *Wall Street Journal.* They selected a large random sample of almost 18% of the articles. Astonishingly,

they found that more than half gave equal weight to the consensus view on the one hand and the scientifically discredited view that human beings play no role in global warming on the other. The authors of this study concluded that American news media had been falsely "giving the impression that the scientific community was embroiled in a rip-roaring debate on whether or not humans were contributing to global warming."[14]

In drawing a conclusion from all this, Gore stated, "No wonder why people are confused." This powerful contrast contains a couple of errors and an omission. Oreskes, who is not a practicing scientist as Gore suggests but is in the Department of History of Science Studies, conducted her study not of *every* peer-reviewed article but of a large random sample based on the key phrase "global climate change." Her brief article in *Science*[15] in 2004 was excerpted from a lecture she had given earlier that year, and that lecture also became the basis of a chapter in a book on climate change that was published in 2007, *Climate Change: What It Means for Us, Our Children and Our Grandchildren*.[16] Gore does not cite the names of the authors of the second study (his book contained no footnotes), but the study he alluded to was generally understood to be written by two brothers, Jules Boykoff, an assistant professor of political science at Pacific University in Forest Grove, Oregon, and Maxwell Boykoff, a research fellow at the University of Oxford's Environmental Change Institute in England. Their study was called "Balance as Bias: Global Warming and the US Prestige Press" and appeared in 2004 in a journal called *Global Environmental Change*.[17]

These mistakes and omissions are minor and only slightly diminish Gore's main point. The earth is getting warmer, and human activities are at least partially to blame. Many Americans believe that scientists are still divided over the issue of global warming when they are not. Politicians, economists, journalists, and others may not be clear, but there is no disagreement among climate scientists.

In her book chapter, Oreskes explained why an analysis of the contents of published scientific papers was so important. These papers "are considered sufficiently supported by evidence that they merit publication in expert journals," she wrote. "The peer review process means that papers published in scientific journals must pass the scrutiny of critical, expert colleagues. They must be supported by sufficient evidence to convince others who know the subject well."[18]

For Oreskes, the unanswered questions are these: How much warmer is the earth getting and how fast is this happening? How widespread will global warming be in the future? But in covering this issue, journalists, hamstrung by the principle of balance, occupy a separate reality. "The mass media has paid a great deal of attention to a handful of dissenters in a manner that is greatly disproportionate with their representation in the scientific community," Oreskes wrote.[19] Most of the dissenters, she said, "are not actually climate scientists" and are not experts on the subjects they opine on: "The vast majority of materials denying the reality of global warming do not pass the most basic test for what it takes to be counted as scientific, namely, being published in a peer-reviewed journal."[20] Oreskes likens these contrarian views to the views of those who promote the reality of UFOs.

The prestige press in particular has contributed to poor understanding of global warming, in the view of the Boykoffs. "These press outlets have done this by adhering to the journalistic norm of balanced reporting, offering a countervailing 'denial discourse'—a voluble minority view that argues that global warming is not scientifically provable or that it is not a serious issue," they wrote.[21] "Balanced reporting can actually be a form of informational bias," they argued, when it comes to coverage of global warming. They found that in the majority of coverage in the "prestige press," balanced accounts prevailed: these accounts gave "roughly equal attention" to the view that humans were contributing to global warming and to the opposing view, that exclusively natural fluctuations could explain the earth's temperature increase.[22]

With echoes reminiscent of the DDT debate involving Jack Devlin, Gore in his book detected sinister motives in those denying global warning. "The misconception that there is serious disagreement among scientists about global warming is actually an illusion that has been deliberately fostered by a relatively small but extremely well-funded cadre of special interests, including Exxon Mobil and a few other oil, coal and utilities companies," he wrote. With more rhetoric than hard evidence, he added: "These companies want to prevent any new policies that would interfere with their current business plans that rely on the massive unrestrained dumping of global warming pollution in the earth's atmosphere every hour of the day."[23]

Stephen Schneider, a highly visible, articulate, and thoughtful Stanford climatologist who moves comfortably in the public arena, has offered a simple but important insight into reporting on scientific issues. Science reporting is different from reporting on current events, he has written on his web page: "There are rarely just two polar opposite sides, but rather a spectrum of potential outcomes, oftentimes accompanied by a considerable history of scientific assessment of the relative credibility of these many possibilities," he wrote. "A climate scientist faced with a reporter locked into the 'get both sides' mind-set risks getting his or her views stuffed into one of two boxed storylines: 'we're worried' or 'it will all be OK.' And sometimes, these two 'boxes' are misrepresentative; a mainstream, well-established consensus may be 'balanced' against the opposing views of a few extremists, and to the uninformed, each position seems equally credible. Any scientist wandering into the political arena and naively thinking 'balanced' assessment is what all sides seek (or hear) had better learn fast how the advocacy system really functions."[24]

For journalists to improve, Schneider suggested, they must "replace the knee-jerk model of 'journalistic balance' with a more accurate and fairer doctrine of perspective that communicates not only the range of opinion, but also the relative credibility of each opinion within the scientific community. Just as a good scientist records and analyzes all relevant data before reaching conclusions, a good reporter will not just take a story at face value, but will delve deep into the issue to ensure accuracy and see how many varying opinions there truly are." The best science and environmental reporters have already abandoned the idea of reporting both sides, he observed, but this model of reporting still exists in the political arena. When political reporters cover science, Schneider wrote, "they typically revert to form: equally credible polar opposites." For him, most emphatically, not all opinions deserve equal billing.

What is needed to properly inform the public is what Schneider has called a "perspectives approach," in which journalists elaborate the relative credibility of many views on complex issues, not just the extreme opposites. Author John Hersey proclaimed that the legend on the journalistic license must read: "None of this was made up." Perhaps a corollary should be added: "Not every story has two sides."

—————————◇—————————

FIVE

EYEWITNESS TO HISTORY

Long before there was social science, long before there was journalism, William Shakespeare wrote enduring plays. In Hamlet in
1601, Shakespeare pinpointed the flaws of eyewitness testimony
and wryly commented on the power of suggestion. Polonius ar-
rives on stage, telling Prince Hamlet that his mother, the queen,
wishes to see him.

Hamlet deflects the question:

> *Hamlet:* Do you see yonder cloud that's almost in shape of a
> camel?
> *Polonius:* By th' mass, and 'tis, like a camel indeed.
> *Hamlet:* Methinks it is like a weasel.
> *Polonius:* It is back'd like a weasel.
> *Hamlet:* Or like a whale.
> *Polonius:* Very like a whale.[1]

Centuries later, Fernand van Langenhove, a Belgian sociologist,
began his book *The Growth of a Legend* with an old German
proverb: "When war visits a country, lies become as numerous as
grains of sand."[2] Van Langenhove, in exploring the misreporting
of German atrocities against Belgian civilians in 1914, discussed at
length the errors that may be made in describing the "observed
fact."[3] The first example he cited was known, in the literature of
the time, as the attempt at murder at Professor Franz V. Liszt's
school of criminology. Two students at the school got into a

heated argument. They insulted and threatened each other until one of the disputants finally fired upon the other at point-blank range. Students who were present were later called as witnesses and asked to write accounts of what had happened. Some were instructed to write their accounts on the day of the incident. Others were asked to write up their recollections the following day. Still others were asked a week afterward, three weeks afterward, or five weeks afterward. The witnesses were law students in their final year and were thought to be people of a certain sophistication and "maturity of judgment."[4]

The attempted murder was, in fact, an experiment that had been arranged to the smallest detail without the students' knowledge. The examination of the "witnesses" revealed that none of them was entirely correct. Memories of the early stages of the argument were inaccurate, but once one of the disputants threatened the other with a fist, the extent of the errors increased. Presumably the threat increased the excitement of the spectators, clouding their perceptions.

Van Langenhove then recounted another experiment that was originally described by Arnold von Gennep, a noted ethnographer who is recognized as the founder of the field of folklore in France. In his book *La formation des legends,* von Gennep related the following experiment that took place at a Congress of Psychology in Göttingen before a crowd of presumably trained observers:

> Not far from the hall in which the Congress was sitting there was a public fete with a masked ball. Suddenly the door of the hall was thrown open and a clown rushed in madly pursued by a negro, revolver in hand. They stopped in the middle of the room fighting; the clown fell, the negro leapt upon him, fired, and then

both rushed out of the hall. The whole incident hardly lasted twenty seconds.

The president asked those present to write immediately a report since there was sure to be a judicial enquiry. Forty reports were sent in. Only one had less than 20 percent of mistakes in regard to the principal facts; fourteen had 20 percent to 40 percent of mistakes; twelve from 40 percent to 50 percent; thirteen more than 50 percent. Moreover in twenty-four accounts, 10 percent of the details were pure inventions and this proportion was exceeded in ten accounts and diminished in six. Briefly, a quarter of the accounts were false.

It goes without saying that the whole scene had been arranged and even photographed in advance. The ten false reports may then be relegated to the category of tales and legends; twenty-four accounts are half legendary, and six have a value approximating to exact evidence.[5]

Van Langenhove ascribed the errors of the eyewitnesses to four factors, which may be summarized as follows:

1. The emotional condition of the observer: the extent of errors increased in proportion to the observer's excitement.
2. Unfamiliarity: the less familiar the situation is, the higher the error rate.
3. The predispositions of the spectators regarding the incident or the people taking part in it.
4. The time that elapsed for the spectators between witnessing the incident and giving their account: the longer the time, the less accurate the recollection.

"It would be absurd and unjustifiable," van Langenhove concluded, "to deduce that the observation of a fact can never lead to exact knowledge of it, but it follows . . . that before being accepted as true a statement as to something seen requires rigorous criticism."[6]

In his influential 1922 book, *Public Opinion,* Walter Lippmann cited the von Gennep experiment, as described by Van Langenhove, and concluded: "Thus out of 40 trained observers writing a responsible account of a scene that had just happened before their eyes, more than a majority saw a scene that had not taken place. What then did they see? One would suppose it was easier to tell what had occurred, than to invent something which had not occurred. They saw their stereotype of such a brawl. All of them had in the course of their lives acquired a series of images of brawls, and these images flickered before their eyes. In one man these images displaced less than 20 per cent of the actual scene, in 13 men more than half. In 34 out of the 40 observers the stereotypes pre-empted at least one tenth of the scene."[7]

Similar experiments have been repeated countless times. In another celebrated story of half a century ago, New York City newspapers reported a woman's assault on a Russian statesman, Alexander K., at a theater. According to the *New York Daily News,* she struck him on the left cheek with her bouquet. The *New York Times* indicated that she slapped his face three times with her gloves. The *Mirror* described a single blow.

More recently, Edna Buchanan, the acclaimed police reporter for the *Miami Herald,* updated the experiment in a shooting scenario that she staged in the classroom for her students in a crime-reporting class at Florida International University. Midway through her lecture, her friend Ann entered as planned, clutched Buchanan's arm, and pleaded for help: "There's been a terrible accident. I've got to find my son and take him home." Then another friend, D. P., burst in through another door, snatched Buchanan's handbag off the desk, and fled. Students began to pursue both Ann and D. P.[8]

And then Buchanan ended the charade: "Freeze! Nobody move!" She told the students they had fifteen minutes to write down what had happened. "The lesson," Buchanan later observed, "was in eyewitness identification, so beloved by juries, so often inaccurate." Unsurprisingly, the written accounts by the students diverged widely. For instance, Buchanan's friend Ann is tall, with shoulder-length dark hair, and she had worn a green print jumpsuit. One of Buchanan's students described Ann as a "petite blond in a miniskirt." The students' description of D. P.'s height ranged from five feet six inches to six feet two inches.

For twenty years, I have used such classroom exercises in a lecture course I teach, and so I was particularly interested in Buchanan's experiment, which she described in an op-ed article in the *New York Times* in the May 25, 1991, issue. (I had clipped this article, so it is readily at hand. It is unavailable in the *New York Times* electronic archive, an example of how even recent history can be distorted in the electronic age.) In my experiment, which I usually base on scripts, students get names wrong and are often far off in their descriptions of weight, height, and hair color. Rarely do they accurately recall what was said.

As instructive as these exercises are in showing journalists or journalism students that eyewitness testimony can be seriously flawed, most of the available research on eyewitness testimony relates to the criminal justice system. A leading researcher on this topic today is Gary Wells of the psychology department of Iowa State University. In an academic paper he published in 2003 with his colleague Elizabeth Olson, the authors noted:

> Eyewitnesses are critical in solving crimes, and sometimes eye-witness testimony is the only evidence available for determining the identity of the culprit. Psychological researchers who began programs in the 1970s, however, have consistently articulated concerns about the accuracy of eyewitness identification. Using various methodologies, such as filmed events and live staged crimes, eyewitness researchers have noted that mistaken identification rates can be surprisingly high and that eyewitnesses often express certainty when they mistakenly select someone from a lineup.[9]

In the late 1990s, as forensic DNA tests emerged, the fallibility of eyewitness testimony was highlighted. By the end of the decade, more than 100 people who had been convicted before the advent of forensic DNA were exonerated, and three-quarters of those people had been victims of mistaken eyewitness identification.[10]

Most crimes, however, leave no DNA traces, and eyewitness identification for solving crimes remains critically important. Since journalists do not have ready access to DNA testing, fingerprinting, or lie detectors, their reliance on their eyes remains undiminished. But journalists are doubly hexed: in the first place, they are rarely in a position to witness something firsthand. More often than not, reports reconstruct events from eyewitness accounts, as illustrated by this compelling lead that Seth Mydans wrote from Bangkok in 2006 for the *International Herald Tribune:*

> Jesse Lee Daniel had just called for mustard for his chicken burger when the first bomb went off with a thud strong enough to shake the Swan Bar, where he was sitting in the southern city of Hat Yai. After the second bomb last Saturday evening 100 yards away at the Odeon department store, he hurried out with other foreign

teachers who had been eating at the bar to take a look. He was standing in front of the New Cherry Ancient Massage parlor, in a crowd of onlookers and masseuses, when the third bomb exploded on a motorbike parked at the curb beside them. Mr. Daniel, a Canadian, died instantly.[11]

Mydans did not have to be at the scene to reconstruct the awful events later. He presumably talked to Jesse Lee Daniel's colleagues in order to give Daniel's perspective of his own death.

Second, even when they are in a position to witness something firsthand, reporters may fall victim to the hazards of eyewitness testimony. They may not remember all the details. They may seriously miscalculate how long an incident lasted. They may have misunderstood what people were saying or doing. Yet eyewitness testimony surely can be correct, and skilled people are much better at it than amateurs.

The fallibility of eyewitness observation plays into the postmodern sensibility in which individual, subjective understandings have as much validity as universal truths. In postmodernism, there is no universal truth. What you think depends on your own experience and what you pay attention to. What you think is as valid as what anyone else thinks. For a long time, according to Mitchell Stephens, one of the leading thinkers about journalists, journalists "were content to ignore postmodernism—a loose collection of philosophical ideas and aesthetic notions that have in common a revolt against the belief that any one perspective, any one view of reality, has ultimate priority."[12] With the arrival of the twenty-first century, "the notion that 'it's all spin'—that, as deconstruction and other postmodern theories have long argued, interpretation is inextricably bound with reality—has not only gained a foothold in journalism; it threatens to take over journalism."[13]

Stephens advocated a journalism of openness: "Journalists should acknowledge, as postmodernists are always eager to do, the complications. But they should still provide their audiences with as much of the information needed to make a judgment as possible. They should take their audiences as close as possible to truth."[14] In his article, Stephens approvingly cited a 6,700-word article by Mark Danner on the election in Iraq that was published in the *New York Review of Books* in April 2005. Danner showed how intense security concerns, particularly the fear of kidnapping, had "driven reporters off the streets," and he argued that this had reduced them to practicing "hotel journalism." Danner wrote:

> As suicide bombers and kidnappers created the new concrete city, they have driven reporters off the streets, away from the restaurants and shops, away from "ordinary Iraqis," forcing them to sheath themselves in flak jackets and helmets, move in armored cars, and finally take refuge behind blast walls and barbed wire and armed guards in fortress-like hotels. Television reporters, politically the most important journalists on the ground—for they supply information, and above all images, to by far the largest number of people—are in practical terms the most vulnerable; their large "footprint"—the cameras and other equipment they carry, the crews they bring to carry it—makes them most conspicuous, and thus most restricted.[15]

Danner took his audience behind the scenes: "The correspondent you watch signing off his nightly report from the war zone with his name, network, and dateline 'Baghdad' is usually speaking from the grounds or the roof of a fully guarded, barricaded hotel—a virtual high-rise bunker—and may not have ventured out of that hotel all day, having spent his time telephoning, reading the wires, and scrutinizing footage from Iraqi 'stringers' who have been out on the street. When he does leave the hotel it will be in an armored car, surrounded by armed security guards, and very likely the destination will be a news conference or briefing or arranged interview in the vast American-ruled bunker known as 'the Green Zone.'"

Danner himself did not hide the fact that he had walked the streets only once on this visit—on Election Day itself—and then was able to visit only two polling places. "Hotel journalism" has long had a bad odor to it, in wars past and in spoofs of wars past, most notably in Evelyn Waugh's satire of war correspondents, *Scoop* (not to be confused with Woody Allen's 2006 movie by the same name).

Sorties beyond Baghdad, Danner continued, "or even to 'hot' neighborhoods within the capital, can usually be undertaken only by 'embedding' with American troops. It is a bizarre, dispiriting way to work, this practice of 'hotel journalism,' producing not only a highly constrained picture of the country and its politics but, on the part of the journalist, constant fear, anxiety, and ultimately intense frustration. 'I am getting out of here, getting out soon,' one network correspondent told me. When I asked why—for American foreign correspondents Iraq is, after all, the most important story going—he shrugged: 'It's no longer honest work.'"[16] (Danner's reporting closely echoed the perceptions of many of the full-time war correspondents in Iraq. Six months before Danner wrote his piece, Farnaz Fassihi, the *Wall Street Journal*'s Middle East correspondent, became the focus of unwanted attention after she sent an e-mail to her close friends summarizing with candid eloquence the frustration of reporting in a modern war zone. The e-mail circulated far beyond her intended audience when one of her friends published it online. The e-mail said, in part:

Being a foreign correspondent in Baghdad these days is like being under virtual house arrest. Forget about the reasons that lured me to this job: a chance to see the world, explore the exotic, meet new people in far away lands, discover their ways and tell stories that could make a difference.

Little by little, day-by-day, being based in Iraq has defied all those reasons. I am house bound. I leave when I have a very good reason to and a scheduled interview. I avoid going to people's homes and never walk in the streets. I can't go grocery shopping any more, can't eat in restaurants, can't strike up a conversation with strangers, can't look for stories, can't drive in anything but a full armored car, can't go to scenes of breaking news stories, can't be stuck in traffic, can't speak English outside, can't take a road trip, can't say I'm an American, can't linger at checkpoints, can't be curious about what people are saying, doing, feeling. And can't and can't. There has been one too many close calls, including a car bomb so near our house that it blew out all the windows. So now my most pressing concern every day is not to write a kick-ass story but to stay alive and make sure our Iraqi employees stay alive. In Baghdad I am a security personnel first, a reporter second.[17]

The Iraq War represents a decisive change for reporters who cover wars. Covering battles is difficult and terrifying enough. This war became the most thoroughly reported war in modern times and has been a live, real-time war, with Western reporters becoming fair game for the enemy in a way that never happened before. It became the most dangerous war ever for journalists.

On-the-scene, eyewitness reporting of wars is a comparatively recent phenomenon. "The decision by *The Times* of London in 1854 to send a general reporter to the Crimean War marked an immense leap in the history of journalism," noted Phillip Knightley in the revised edition of *The First Casualty: The War Correspondent as Hero and Myth-Maker from the Crimea to Iraq,* his authoritative, if quirky, history of war coverage. Knightley wrote:

> But from the very beginning, war correspondents faced a dilemma that remains unresolved to this day: Whose side are they on? Correspondents have to choose because the aims of the military and the media are irreconcilable. The military wants to win the war as quickly as possible and preferably, because the face of battle is horrific, away from the public eye. The media wants to observe the military in action, bear witness, and record the first draft of history. If doing this as accurately and as truthfully as possible means writing and broadcasting stories damaging to their nation's war effort, what are correspondents to do? Does the journalist within the correspondent prevail? Or the patriot? And what if reporting patriotically involves telling lies? Is that journalism or propaganda?[18]

Knightley took the title of his book from the phrase attributed to California Senator Hiram Johnson, a staunch isolationist who when the United States entered World War I, noted in an unrecorded speech in the Senate, "The first casualty, when war comes, is truth." (In the *Idler* in 1758, Samuel Johnson had voiced a similar sentiment: "Among the calamities of war may be justly numbered the diminution of the love of truth, by the falsehoods which interest dictates and credulity encourages."[19])

When Knightley wrote the first edition of his book more than thirty years ago, he wished "to record how war had been reported through the ages and to highlight the unforgiving verdict of history on those reports." In most cases, he discovered, "journalism, meant to be the first draft of history, had to be substantially redrafted as hindsight revealed that important parts of the story had been omitted or twisted."[20]

In the postmodern spirit, many close readers have a favorite reporter. Mine became Ian Fisher of the *New York Times.* I know little about him. To my knowledge I have never met him or been in the same room with him. Fisher brought a different, elegant, highly self-aware sensibility to his coverage. In an article in the summer of 2004, he recorded how Western reporters in Baghdad were frustrated, unable to see with their own eyes what was happening nearby, "most of us having been locked down in Baghdad for months." Fisher wrote that reporters were

> beginning to think what it might mean to get out and cover more of Iraq again, and see first-hand whether things are improving or getting worse. For months it has been too dangerous for obviously Western reporters to spend time in places like Sadr City, the biggest slum in Iraq, or Falluja, now a safe haven for Iraqi insurgents and outright terrorists. Around the country, reporters were kidnapped, chased and threatened. A few were killed. Paul D. Wolfowitz, the deputy defense secretary, complained that we were too scared to tell the whole story of Iraq. It felt to us like a cheap shot, but he got it half right: We were scared, and we, too, wondered how we could possibly cover America's biggest story since Vietnam without the most basic security.[21]

The reporters were facing a Hobson's choice, which was really no choice at all. It was impossible to see anything very much first-hand, and therefore the primary source became the American military, which was "fine for what it is," Fisher wrote, "but not nearly enough to assemble the full picture." The irony was palpable. "The people who write and those who appear in front of cameras no longer could report on events they saw with their own eyes—

as flawed as that might be," he said. As an alternative, Western news organizations began to rely on their Arab and Iraqi staff members, who could go almost anywhere. Some were trained reporters, Fisher wrote. Others were just people who spoke English and were willing to put their lives at risk for the Westerners who employed them. "We at the *Times,*" Fisher pointed out, "have been able to see Iraq through the eyes of an Iraqi housewife, a college student and a veteran of the Iran-Iraq war, and others who came from professional careers. Using them has helped Western reporters to see the news as Iraqis do—often fact by fact, each excruciatingly excavated by debriefing people who are not really trained to collect news."

A few months earlier, Fisher had written a brilliantly crafted, understated piece about a roadside bomb that killed a young American soldier on a Sunday morning in Baghdad in April 2004. It was, Fisher noted, "the kind of attack so common in this war it no longer makes headlines."[22] But, with insight and uncommon sensitivity, he wrote this story so evocatively that it appeared on page one. After the dead soldier was evacuated, his Humvee was set on fire and children rushed to the street to celebrate. Rooftop snipers appeared, and American soldiers began shooting at them, killing at least one Iraqi teenager who was caught in the cross-fire.

"Those details, at least, seem certain enough," Fisher wrote, on deadline, in a calm, straightforward tone. He had arrived on the scene about six hours after the killing, and, for safety considerations, was able to stay for only about forty-five minutes. "Determining the truth of what happened in incidents like this one is becoming increasingly difficult," Fisher wrote. "Reality, at this pivotal moment for the Americans in Iraq, is a kaleidoscope of versions."

In his account, Iraqi witnesses said not one child, but four or possibly five, had been killed. The American military had no count. But according to the military, gunmen had fired on the soldiers from rooftops, provoking return fire. No Iraqi witness mentioned Iraqis firing first. Several Iraqis on the scene said the children had been incited to jump around the burning Humvee by a cameraman for Al Arabiya, the Arab news channel, which, Fisher wrote, "American officials say is guilty of stoking a much broader anti-Americanism among viewers around the Arab world." When reached for comment, the news channel denied the accusation and said its cameraman just filmed the incident.

The multiple versions of truth and the uncertainty of factual accuracy at the crime scene are eerily reminiscent of *Rashomon,* the 1950 Japanese motion-picture masterpiece directed by Akira Kurosawa and starring Toshiro Mifune. In the film, the story of a rape and murder unfolds in flashbacks that supply the widely different accounts of four eyewitnesses—the bandit, the murdered samurai, his wife, and a woodcutter. Each witness contradicts the others. The movie's theme is the impossibility of figuring out the truth about an event from conflicting accounts of people who were presumably present. *Rashomon* has become almost a code word to describe a situation where eyewitnesses are so at odds in their retelling of what happened that truth slips away. The movie has had enduring influence in many levels of our culture. In 2006, for instance, *Hoodwinked,* an animated movie, used the format of multiple perspectives to retell the fable of Little Red Riding Hood. Finally, "a *Rashomon* for the whole family," wrote a movie critic for the *Village Voice,* who found the updated version boring.[23]

In his contemporary *Rashomon,* Fisher in the *Times* presented several accounts of the roadside bombing and its aftermath, asserting that "the contradictory versions of what happened seem revealing about the thickening fog of this war."

First, there was Qusay Faisal, nineteen, who said he had been standing across the Canal highway in the Amana neighborhood of northeastern Baghdad. He claimed that he had seen four American Humvees drive by on the other side of the road. He said a friend, Khalid, about thirty, had run up to them and fired a rocket-propelled grenade that hit one Humvee. Soldiers, Faisal said, aided their colleagues from the damaged Humvee, while others left their vehicles and began firing. Pointing to "dusty spatters" of blood, Faisal said that Khalid was struck as he attempted to escape across a bridge over a sewage canal. Only one other youth, Hussein, Faisal said, had been shot by the American bullets, sustaining a wound in the leg. Faisal saw no other killings. "The Americans did a good thing when they captured Saddam Hussein," Fisher quoted Faisal as saying. "But why do they kill children? Before, I liked the Americans, but now I hate them." Further complicating Faisal's testimony, Fisher noted, is that Faisal had admitted that he had been drinking when the attack happened. No one corroborated what Faisal claimed to have seen.

From a different vantage point, across the highway, Jabal Shanoon Hussain, forty-two, a sergeant at the fire station, said, when interviewed, that he had heard a huge explosion from several hundred yards away and had seen the four Humvees stopping. He saw what looked like wounded soldiers being transferred to other Humvees before the vehicles drove away. Then, Hussain said, youths from the nearby Sakir Quraish Middle School streamed toward the Humvees, celebrating the attack, and about ten minutes later several other American Humvees arrived, and the soldiers inside opened fire. Hussain said that he had seen the body of his young neighbor, Hassan. He saw only one other wounded person, a child, about four years old.

Behind the firehouse, Fisher saw workers erecting a steel-framed tent, which in the Arab world is used for funerals. "Two neighbors corroborated Mr. Hussain's account that the stricken Humvee seemed to have been hit by a bomb several hundred yards from where it had stopped," Fisher reported. "They also agreed that a second group of Americans began shooting after arriving and finding the burning Humvee—and did so wildly." In an example of flawed hearsay evidence, the neighbors said that they had heard that four children had been killed, but they had not seen the bodies themselves.

Muhammad Yacut, forty, said that he arrived just after the explosion to see scores of youths near the bridge and a cameraman he believed to be from Al Arabiya, who, he said, was urging the youths to celebrate. Fisher wrote: "The cameraman said, 'Come over the bridge and celebrate, and I will film you,' Mr. Yacut said in an account supported by others in the neighborhood." Yacut said that a taxi driver had poured gasoline over the Humvee and set it on fire. Then a second group of Americans arrived, Yacut said, and opened fire. He said he had seen four or five children lying still, presumably dead.

Later, at Sadr General Hospital, surgeon Muaed Aad said the hospital had received fourteen wounded but no fatalities. However, it is also true, added Fisher, that Iraqis, observing the Muslim tradition of immediate burial, often do not take the dead to hospitals.

Then there was the official American version. The chief military spokesman, Brigadier General Mark Kimmitt, reported that, on Sunday, one soldier had been killed and three wounded by a roadside bomb. According to Fisher's account, "when soldiers returned to their Humvees after evacuating wounded soldiers, they found children rifling through the vehicles, and gunmen began firing from rooftops. General Kimmitt suggested that American soldiers, who returned fire, had not caused any injuries or deaths."

"We strongly suspect the shooting from the rooftops was responsible for any casualties," General Kimmitt told reporters, adding that the incident was under investigation. Fisher telephoned the Baghdad bureau chief for Al Arabiya, Hisham Badawi, and Badawi said that a freelance cameraman who often worked for the network was at the scene and had been arrested by American troops. He said that the cameraman, Aqeel Muhammad, had not encouraged the children to celebrate the destroyed Humvee.

Fisher did not sort out his *Rashomon*-like tale. He could not. But it endures as eloquent testimony to the abiding issue of trying to discover truth in war from a welter of conflicting versions of truth.

SIX

TABLOID TRUTHS

The tabloid that has long been a fixture in our culture, the *National Enquirer,* was in a tailspin by the summer of 2001. At first, it became a victim of its own success. Starting in 1989, a series of new owners had paid a steep premium, and they carried a heavy debt. The only way to make the paper profitable was to reduce staff, thus eliminating some of the very reporters who had made the tabloid successful in the first place. In addition, the *Enquirer* had spawned many imitators, and that competition had affected circulation, which had plummeted. This, in turn, had led to more cost-cutting measures. The tabloid's budget was tight. The company was about to hire a new, less expensive law firm to represent it. But what had worked so well for so many years—using lawyers to read every word in advance, not so much to guarantee literal accuracy but to assure the editors their stories would withstand a libel lawsuit—proved not to be foolproof.

The vicissitudes of the *Enquirer* offer a window into understanding the thin line that often divides the tabloids from the mainstream media. While righteously deploring the tabloids on the one hand, the mainstream press has on the other hand occasionally profited by adopting some of the controversial practices that tabloids have traditionally followed.

That summer of 2001, before the September 11 terrorist attacks, was a time when international issues were a remote concern. The memorable story of that summer turned out to be the hunt for a missing Washington intern, Chandra Levy, who worked for a California congressman, Gary Condit. Condit had been largely unknown outside of his home state until he found himself in the center of the media vortex. At first, Chandra Levy's disappearance was not the *Enquirer*'s type of story. Following a time-tested marketing formula, the *Enquirer* focused its efforts on celebrities—people *already* known to its audience. But soon enough, with the participation of cable television, Gary Condit and Chandra Levy became familiar names, and the *Enquirer* pounced on the story.

In midsummer, the *Enquirer* reported on its website that Gary Condit's wife, Carolyn, a religious woman who avoided publicity, had telephoned her husband's Washington, D.C., apartment from their Ceres, California, home and had spoken to and verbally attacked Chandra Levy during a five-minute telephone conversation. The *Enquirer* reported that the phone call took place just days before Levy's disappearance on May 1, 2001.

On July 28, after the item appeared on the paper's website, a high police official in Washington said: "I don't think there's any truth to that whatsoever."[1] The Washington police issued a second categorical denial. Disregarding these warning signs, the *Enquirer* published an article billed a "world exclusive" in its print edition with the cover date August 7. An oversized headline carried no qualifier: "Cops: Condit's Wife Attacked Chandra."[2]

The first paragraph read: "Gary Condit's bitter wife flew into a rage and attacked Chandra Levy in a furious confrontation just days before the intern's disappearance, the *Enquirer* has learned exclusively." Later the story said: "In a major breakthrough, investigators have uncovered what they say is the 'blowup phone call' between Chandra and Carolyn Condit—during which the 24-year-old intern told an enraged Carolyn that Gary was dumping her to start a new life and family with Chandra."

All these assertions turned out to be utterly false.

In deconstructing the story, we find it contains three objective statements that could have been subjected to verification:

1. Sometime before April 28, 2001, Carolyn Condit called her husband's Washington apartment.
2. Chandra Levy, in the apartment alone, saw that the caller identification was from Condit's California home and answered the call. (This assumes an answering machine with a caller identification feature.)
3. Investigators obtained phone records showing that the phone call in question lasted more than five minutes.

The article also contained a series of subjective characterizations, including:

1. Carolyn Condit was "bitter" and "flew into a rage" in a "furious" confrontation with Levy.
2. The showdown was "brazen."
3. The phone conversation was "heated."
4. In answering the phone, Levy's "blatant" response broke a key rule of Condit's—not to answer the phone.

Clearly, the best sources for this story would have been the participants in the phone conversation. However, Levy disappeared soon after the exchange was supposed to have taken place, and Mrs. Condit, who was never interviewed by the *Enquirer,* claimed that the conversation did not take place. Logically, then, the only way investigators could have known about the conversation would be if Levy had spoken to someone—presumably family members or friends—about it before her disappearance. If, in fact, that happened, the investigators would already be two steps removed from the event. The very best they could have done was to obtain information via an interview with someone to whom one of the participants had spoken—in other words, through hearsay many times removed.

But this was *not* the basis for the *Enquirer*'s story. According to *Enquirer* editor Steve Coz, in a sworn deposition he gave in connection with a libel lawsuit Carolyn Condit brought against the paper, the story was confirmed by a personal friend. According to the Coz deposition, this source, who was on retainer to provide information to the *Enquirer,* presumably had spoken to the chief of the Washington police, who in turn had obtained inside information from his investigators. This makes the central sources of the story four steps removed from directly knowing what could have happened—an untenably shaky connection.

In his deposition, Coz, almost always referred to as the "Harvard-trained" editor, was asked about the standards of the *Enquirer.* Coz said that he believed they were "the same standards as any other newspapers would be held to. In other words, we would go through the same diligent process with our information that any newspaper would go through, to feel totally comfortable that the information we're printing is true. There are no shortcuts, no recklessness or negligence. We take our work very, very seriously."

But in this instance, at least, the reporting of the *Enquirer* led it far astray from the truth, and the standards that Coz testified to were nowhere to be found. In her complaint, Mrs. Condit's lawyers averred: "Mrs. Condit has never seen Miss Levy in person or spoken to her on the telephone. Mrs. Condit's telephone records do not reflect a five-minute or any phone call made 'days before' Miss Levy's disappearance that was supposedly initiated from their home."

In the past, Coz's source, who had been paid for information by the *Enquirer,* had proved to be reliable. But not this time. Paying for information, in this instance, backfired. Had the *Enquirer* leveled with its readers about its sources, according to Coz's version of events, the hypothetical story might have read something like this: "A friend of the editor who has been a paid informant to the tabloid said that he talked to the police chief who said investigators had interviewed people who told of a heated conversation they did not witness between Ms. Levy and Mrs. Condit. The police officials deny that they know of such a conversation. Mrs. Condit was not reached for comment, but has told others no such conversation took place. The *Enquirer* has not seen the phone records mentioned in the story, and it has no independent knowledge that Gary Condit has an answering machine."

That, of course, is no story at all.

As it turned out, according to the key source's version of events when he was deposed, Coz totally misunderstood what the source had told him. This is how a hypothetical version of the informant's story would begin: "A friend and source of the editor said the police chief told him that there was an unconfirmed rumor—one of many unconfirmed rumors—among his officers that a heated conversation took place between two women . . ."

That would be even less of a story.

Surely neither of these imagined versions in any way supports the headline or first paragraph of the *actual* story—that Carolyn Condit "attacked" Chandra Levy. This incident underscores an unfortunate aspect of journalism: doing more reporting may in fact demolish a good tale, and sometimes reporters are reluctant to ruin stories. Had the *Enquirer*'s reporters done more interviewing, sourcing, and checking, they would have discovered that this "attack" never took place. Coz's confidence in his informant, as a confirming source, was spectacularly misplaced.

At the end of the story it did run, the *Enquirer* included a boilerplate hedge. The final paragraph contained this disclaimer: "The source close to the case added: 'No one is suggesting Carolyn is guilty of anything—but investigators believe she could be the key to learning the events that may have precipitated Chandra's disappearance.'"

But this language—"No one is suggesting Carolyn is guilty of anything"—hardly mitigates what preceded it. The reader is left wondering. Guilty of what? Suggested by whom?

I became involved in this case as a paid expert witness retained by the lawyers for Mrs. Condit. As part of my duties, I submitted a written report in which I underscored a reality that is one of the central themes of this book. Eyewitness reporting occurs infrequently. Only rarely do reporters directly observe a crime as it happens. Almost never are they inside a room when an important policy decision is made. That means many stories are secondhand at best. When applicable, a news story should make evident that a narrative of an event was reconstructed from later interviews or derived from documents. If journalists reconstruct quotations or re-create events they did not witness, best practices require that the audience should know that these specific quotations or events were reconstructed and how they were confirmed. The further removed reporters are from seeing the event or hearing the precise words, the greater the burden on reporters to reveal the chain of evidence. Reporters should indicate how direct the source's knowledge is and what biases the source might have. Due credit must be given to conflicting views.

Hours after I gave my oral deposition, which was based on my written report, the lawsuit was settled, and coincidentally or not, Steve Coz left his editor's job soon after. As is customary in such cases, the terms of the settlement were not disclosed. I gather, however, that neither Carolyn Condit nor her husband will ever have to work again.

I have long had a fascination with the *Enquirer* and its role in contemporary journalism. The Graduate School of Journalism at the University of California at Berkeley, where I have taught on and off for many years, benefited from an earlier settlement of a lawsuit involving the *Enquirer*. Carol Burnett sued the tabloid and donated part of the money she was awarded in the settlement to the university. Another connection to the *Enquirer* occurred when I was a reporter for *New York Newsday* in 1987. Prompted by the *Enquirer*'s publication of a picture of presidential candidate Gary Hart with Donna Rice on his lap on a pleasure vessel named *Monkey Business,* I visited Lantana, Florida, the *Enquirer*'s headquarters, and wrote a long profile of the paper.[3] And five years later, in 1992, I invited *Enquirer* president Iain Calder, who was on a West Coast goodwill tour, to give a talk at Berkeley. He gave a well-received slideshow presentation in which he argued that the covers of the *Enquirer* were more akin to those of *People* than anything else, and that in fact, the *Enquirer* was ahead of *People* in celebrity coverage. At one time, a colleague from my reporting days at the *New York Times* was a part-owner of the paper. Later, an acquaintance of mine, former U.S. Treasury official Roger Altman, headed the investment group, Evercore Partners, that purchased the parent company of the paper. I had been retained in the Carolyn Condit matter by Neville Johnson, a Berkeley graduate who had become a successful plaintiff's lawyer in Los Angeles.

The modern *Enquirer* traces its heritage to 1924 and to Bernarr McFadden, a skinny, sickly child who transformed himself into a man obsessed with physical fitness and his physique. McFadden founded the *New York Evening Graphic,* which had screaming headlines and embellished the news. Its "composographs" were photos where the faces of famous people were superimposed on the bodies of actors posed in reenactment scenes. "We intend to interest you mightily," McFadden wrote. "We intend to dramatize and sensationalize the news and some stories that are not news."[4] The newspaper's format was that of a tabloid—half the size of a traditional broadsheet. Its staples were crime stories, lurid pictures, photos of almost naked women, and bizarre tales. Like today's supermarket tabloids, it carried nothing resembling standard news.

In this milieu, the *Enquirer* was founded by a former Hearst advertising executive in 1926 as a full-size Sunday paper. In 1952 the paper was bought by Generoso Pope, Jr., for $75,000. Pope was the son of a New York businessman who had published the Italian-language paper *Il Progresso* and owned a radio station. The younger Pope tried various formats for the paper before settling on gore. "I noticed how auto accidents drew crowds and I decided that if it was blood that interested people, I'd give it to them," Pope reminisced.[5] Without shame, the paper focused on the macabre and built its circulation on stories of horrible murders and accidents, vicious gossip columns, and melodramatic stories. The original *Enquirer* ran stories about two-headed babies and headless torsos and aliens from outer space.

In the late 1960s, Pope decided on a new approach. As freestanding newsstands died out, Pope turned to supermarkets, a yet untried outlet for newspapers and periodicals. For figuring out this new marketing approach, the Harvard Business School website hails Pope as one of the "Great American Business Leaders" of the twentieth century. While the *National Enquirer* "is most known for its outlandish stories, Pope is heralded in the publishing world for creating an elaborate and highly profitable distribution network," the website notes. "He successfully courted the large supermarket chains by offering a generous revenue-sharing model—one that would become a new standard."[6]

Pope began appealing to middle-aged housewives who had little formal schooling. In his effort to have the paper distributed in supermarkets, he changed the editorial recipe to focus on celebrities and health issues. He ran features on household repairs and pop psychology mixed with outlandish human-interest stories. The editors studied the Nielsen ratings carefully and scoured the transcripts of daytime soap operas, which they assumed their audience would be watching. They then commissioned stories about popular stars.

A hard edge still marked the paper, and a low point for the *Enquirer* came in 1976 when it published a brief item describing a tipsy Carol Burnett who had supposedly engaged in an argument with Henry Kissinger at a Washington restaurant—when no such event had occurred.[7] The four-sentence gossip item was headlined "Carol Burnett and Henry K in Row" and ran on an inside page. It began with this description of an incident at a Washington restaurant: "A boisterous Carol Burnett had a loud argument with another diner, Henry Kissinger. Then she traipsed around the place offering everyone a bite of her dessert." The story went on to note that "Burnett really raised eyebrows when she accidentally knocked a glass of wine over one diner and started giggling instead of apologizing. The guy wasn't amused and 'accidentally' spilled a glass of water over Carol's dress."

As it came out at trial, the events in question took place in late January 1976 when Burnett and her husband were dining with three friends at Rive Gauche, a high-end Georgetown restaurant.[8] Burnett was in Washington to honor an invitation to perform at the White House. She had had a couple of glasses of wine, but she was in no way inebriated. A young couple seated at the table next to Burnett's were celebrating a birthday. At their request, she passed small amounts of her chocolate soufflé to them. As she was leaving the restaurant, she was introduced to Henry Kissinger. The former secretary of state later testified that he and Burnett were politely introduced and exchanged pleasantries.

Many years later, Iain Calder recalled in his memoir, *The Untold Story: My 20 Years Running the National Enquirer:* "It all seemed fairly tame compared to other types of items we often ran. I suppose a nuclear bomb is also harmless until it explodes."[9] Burnett complained and almost immediately the *Enquirer* ran a retraction: "An item in this column on March 2 erroneously reported that Carol Burnett had an argument with Henry Kissinger at a Washington restaurant and became boisterous, disturbing other guests. We understand these events did not occur, and we are sorry for any embarrassment our report may have caused Miss Burnett."[10] Despite the retraction, Burnett sued, thereby bringing considerably more attention to herself, particularly among her peers, and to her alleged bad behavior than the inconspicuous original item had stirred.

In his recounting of the case, law professor Rodney Smolla suggested that it became a "rallying point, vulcanizing resentment and bitterness toward the *Enquirer* that had obviously been seething for some time."[11] While the Burnett litigation was being fought out, the *Enquirer* printed a story about rumors of an impending divorce between Johnny Carson of the *Tonight Show* and his third wife, Joanna. As Laurence Leamer, Johnny Carson's biographer, retells it, Carson, in an uncharacteristically serious mood on his late-night show, called the story in the *Enquirer* an "absolutely, completely one-hundred percent falsehood." Carson stated that the people who wrote the story were "liars" and, if they wished, could sue him for slander. "You know where I am, gentlemen," Carson said.[12] The studio audience applauded wildly. When asked for her reaction to Carson, Burnett replied, "I thought he was wonderful."[13] (A couple of years later, Carson and his wife did separate.)

A key issue at the Burnett trial was whether the *Enquirer* should be considered a newspaper or a magazine. Under a California statute, once a newspaper issues a retraction of a published story it has learned was false, a successful lawsuit becomes much less likely. Once a retraction is run, a plaintiff has no right to punitive damages—damages that are intended to hurt the wrongdoer, and damages that can add up to substantial sums. The plaintiff is only entitled to actual pecuniary loss. (For instance, Burnett hypothetically would have had to prove that she had lost employment as a result of the gossip item.) Magazines, however, have no such protection, presumably because of longer lead times, which, in theory, give editors more time to correct errors.

On its cover, the *Enquirer* bragged that it had the "Biggest Circulation of any Paper in America." Although it was published just once a week, the *Enquirer* claimed that it was a newspaper for the purposes of the California retraction statute. But a key expert witness—Albert Pickerell, who taught media law courses at the journalism school at the University of California at Berkeley—testified that the *Enquirer* was a magazine, and this view prevailed on appeal. The trial was widely covered, including on cable television, and Carol Burnett was an excellent witness. Calder recalled how "she had the jury laughing, frowning, sad, happy, and angry—whatever and whenever she wanted. She told them how these few gossip-column lines had devastated her because of a history of alcoholism in her family."[14]

The jury awarded her $300,000 in damages for her pain and suffering and $1.3 million in punitive damages. The judge cut the award in half. An appellate court cut it again. The case was finally settled in 1984 for a sum the parties agreed to keep secret. Burnett, who all along said that she was suing for the principle and not for the financial award, gave her settlement money away. She split the award between the journalism program at Berkeley, in gratitude for Pickerell's testimony, and the University of Hawaii, which was near a house she owned. Reflecting on the verdict, Iain Calder later put a positive gloss on the lawsuit: "Despite the temporary pain, life soon continued on as usual, and Carol Burnett's lawsuit ended up doing us a favor. Maybe we *had* been too cavalier on some stories. Maybe we needed a change."[15]

At this critical juncture, the paper began to strive for the kind of journalistic accuracy that discourages libel suits. The paper started a research department to check facts, listen to interview tapes, and set standards for approving stories before publication. A brilliant stroke occurred when the *Enquirer* decided to retain Williams & Connolly, a first-rate law firm based in Washington that specialized in litigation and First Amendment work. Gene Pope's close friend Peter Peterson, the secretary of commerce in the Nixon cabinet and a hugely successful financier, made the introduction to the firm's founder, the legendary Edward Bennett Williams.

From that time on, for the next two decades, the *Enquirer* never lost another libel case in court, even though it most likely settled unpublicized cases out of court. By retaining Williams & Connolly, the *Enquirer* got itself a powerful law firm and instant cachet. Edward Bennett Williams was an adviser to presidents and a member of the National Security Council, owner of the Baltimore Orioles baseball team, and president of the Washington Redskins football franchise. He was an extraordinary courtroom lawyer who had represented Senator Joseph McCarthy, Frank

Costello, Jimmy Hoffa, and Adam Clayton Powell. More important still, he and his firm represented the *Washington Post*. Now, the
Enquirer shared a law firm with the *Post,* the epitome of The Establishment. Williams's biographer, Evan Thomas, aptly titled his
book, *The Man to See.*

Williams's plan was to shut down litigation against the tabloid
by sending at least three or four lawyers from Washington, D.C.,
to Lantana two or three days each week to read each story and column item and look at every photo. The lawyers would have total
access to each story file, including the reporter's original copy, and
could, if necessary, question any reporter or editor they wanted.
In his memoir, Iain Calder described how the relationship
worked: "Editors began to fax early copy to Washington for advance rulings before the attorneys' weekly visit. They also asked
for legal rulings on how to approach stories. For example, we
might want to take a photo in a hospital. How could we get the
picture without invading someone's privacy? Williams & Connolly would tell us."[16]

In other words, no story would appear in the newspaper until
it had been reviewed and approved by Williams & Connolly. That
did *not* mean every story had to be journalistically accurate. It did
mean that the story had to be good enough to withstand a libel
suit. Hiring Williams & Connolly not only allowed the paper to
run shoulder to shoulder with the establishment press, but also
provided an important insurance policy against future missteps like
the one that had occurred in the Burnett case.

By the mid-1980s, David Kendall, an exceptional lawyer in his
own right, began running the *Enquirer* pre-publication review
process for Williams & Connolly. He did so until 2001, when the
Enquirer came under new ownership. In a bit of tongue-in-cheek
boasting, the Williams & Connolly website recited Kendall's

"checkered legal career": "His acquaintance with the legal process began when he was arrested several times (but convicted only once) in Mississippi during the summer of 1964 while attempting to register voters. After studying at Oxford as a Rhodes Scholar, graduating from Yale Law School, and clerking for Supreme Court Justice Byron R. White, he spent five years as associate counsel at the NAACP Legal Defense & Educational Fund, Inc., litigating a variety of civil rights cases and concentrating on defending death penalty cases."[17]

Kendall represented a number of individual and corporate media clients over the years, defending libel, privacy invasion, and copyright suits, fighting subpoenas to news gatherers, and pursuing freedom of information actions. His clients included the *Washington Post, Newsweek, Playboy,* Discovery Communications, *U.S. Medicine,* the *National Review,* local television stations, and individual writers and journalists. He represented the *Post* at trial and on appeal in a marathon libel suit brought by the president of Mobil Oil and his son, which was known as the Tavoulareas case. (The winning appeal was argued by Edward Bennett Williams, who left his sickbed to persuade the federal appeals court in Washington to reverse an earlier opinion.) In a libel suit arising out of the motion picture *Missing,* Kendall successfully defended its director, Constantin Costa-Gavras, and Universal City Studios in the case that established First Amendment protections for docudramas.

Starting in November 1993, Kendall began representing his fellow Yale Law School graduates President and Mrs. Clinton, who were being investigated for their part in a savings and loan matter involving Whitewater Development Company, Inc. He went on to represent the Clintons in other matters, including investigations, civil litigation, and the 1998–1999 impeachment proceedings. For much of the 1990s, Kendall had two primary clients: the President of the United States and his wife, and the *National Enquirer.*

Kendall's representation of the *Enquirer* was not routine. He became an outright booster. In an interview in 2001 with the alumni magazine of his undergraduate alma mater, Wabash College, Kendall noted: "The *Enquirer* is not what people imagine it to be; the people who talk about it often haven't really read it very much. It has done a lot of incredibly good journalistic work."[18] The *Enquirer* may be different from what it was in the 1970s,[19] but the old *Enquirer* still grips the imagination. In the late 1980s, a play, *Bigfoot Stole My Wife,* opened off-Broadway. It consisted of monologues based on tabloid headlines. One skit was entitled: "I Ate My Best Friend's Brains." Compared to that, the contemporary headlines of the *Enquirer* are rather sedate.

The prime example of what Kendall called the *Enquirer's* "incredibly good journalistic work" was its coverage of the rapid decline of Gary Hart, a former Democratic senator who sought the presidency but whose self-destructiveness did him in. Hart, who had made a strong showing in the final stages of the Democratic primary in 1984, had entered the 1988 race very early, in the spring of 1987, ostensibly to give him time to articulate his policy positions. But the press was not interested in policy. It was preoccupied with his relationships with women other than his wife.

In its coverage of Hart, as in its general coverage, the *Enquirer* used a journalistic technique shunned by the mainstream—it paid for information. Yet, as pivotal a role that the *Enquirer* did play in ruining Hart's presidential plans, its influence was surely not so large as *Enquirer* insiders now remember it. In a bit of tabloid hyperbole not justified by facts, Iain Calder boasted in his memoir that "our cover of June 2, 1987 was a story that changed history. It was a 'death blow' to Hart's political career"[20] The cover photo showed Hart sitting on the deck of a boat with a young woman, Donna Rice, on his knee; the pleasure boat was named—unfortunately for him—*The Monkey Business.* He was wearing a T-shirt imprinted with "Monkey Business Crew."

Days before this picture appeared, Hart had dropped out of the race, as a result of stories the *Miami Herald* did publish and of another story the *Washington Post* did *not* publish.[21] The *Washington Post* presented Hart's advisers with evidence it had gathered of a liaison between the candidate and yet another woman—even stronger evidence than the *Herald* had collected about Donna Rice. If Hart continued in the presidential race, his advisers were told, the story would be made public. Hart withdrew.

The *Herald*'s premature exclusive set in motion Hart's collapse, a downfall that occurred with "breathtaking velocity,"[22] in the words of Paul Taylor, the *Washington Post* reporter who, at a nationally televised news conference, had asked Hart point blank if he was an adulterer. The deeply flawed *Herald* story, which ran in the newspaper's late editions on the first Sunday of May, began: "Gary Hart, the Democratic presidential candidate who has dismissed allegations of womanizing, spent Friday night and most of Saturday in his Capitol Hill townhouse with a young woman who flew from Miami and met him. Hart denied any impropriety."[23] At the time the story ran, the *Herald* reporters did not even know the woman's name. They had conducted a brief stakeout of his townhouse. But they left their prey unwatched for several hours in the middle of the night, and they were unaware of a back door through which people could have entered or left the house without being seen from the front.

The story broke fundamental rules of good journalism and fair play and never should have been published when it was, but it did flush out better, more solidly documented stories that appeared later on. The ground rules for reporting changed the week that story ran. The new rules of engagement for political reporting are often traced—erroneously, it turns out—to the spring of 1987 when Hart posed a challenge to E. J. Dionne, then of the *New York Times,* in a long magazine article: "Follow me around. I don't care," Hart said. "I'm serious. If anybody wants to put a tail on me, go ahead. They'd be very bored."[24] By the time those words were published, according to a later account by James Bennet, then of the *New York Times,* "people were already tailing him. They were not bored."[25]

We are still not sure what happened that night at Hart's townhouse. In the heat of the controversy, before he withdrew from the race, Hart charged: "This story was written by reporters who, by their own admission, undertook a spotty surveillance, who reached inaccurate conclusions based on incomplete facts, who, after publishing a false story, now concede they may have gotten it wrong."[26] Tom Fiedler, then the *Herald* political editor and a member of the team that put the story together, and later executive editor of the paper, told reporters that Hart was "misstating the facts."[27] Later, Rice denied that anything untoward had occurred. With neither party admitting to what novelist Henry James had called the *chronique intime,* there was little, if anything, journalists could do to capture the truth, unless they had been prepared to adopt odious and perhaps unlawful techniques such as planting secret cameras or microphones.

At first, surveillance seems like a promising method to discover truth. It gives reporters the advantage of being eyewitnesses to what they are covering. But a stakeout like the one the *Miami Herald* conducted is, in fact, a highly problematic way of obtaining information. Surveillance is ordinarily employed as a law-enforcement tool—most often to monitor a situation to collect data for later use. Surveillance is used to find patterns. It is used to provide leads, not to supply actual proof.[28] The *Herald* unwisely relied on the stakeout for proof of an illicit affair.

It was at this point that the *National Enquirer,* which had been shunned by the mainstream press because of the Burnett case and other intrusions into the lives of celebrities, unintentionally came to its rescue. The *Enquirer* was a latecomer to the Gary Hart story. As we have seen, it had nothing to do with breaking the story of the former senator's dalliances. Nor would the *Enquirer* have wished to do so. "At first," Iain Calder said at the time, "Gary Hart would not have appealed to Missy Smith in Kansas"—the mythical reader the paper was targeting. "She wouldn't have known who he was."[29]

Several weeks earlier, on March 28, Hart had taken an overnight trip from Miami to the Bahamas on an 83-foot luxury yacht called *Monkey Business.* His companion was Donna Rice, who had previously dated Don Johnson, the actor, and Prince Albert of Monaco. Six weeks after their boat trip, Hart had invited Rice to spend the weekend with him in his Capitol Hill townhouse while his wife was in Denver. The *Herald* was tipped off to this meeting by an unidentified source who wanted to sell pictures of the couple. The *Herald* declined on the ground that buying the pictures would be the same as paying for news. It would be checkbook journalism, and the *Herald* would not think of engaging in that practice.

In the week that Hart became universally known, the *Enquirer* got to work. It learned of the existence of the photos that the *Herald* had declined to buy. Although the pictures did not show anything particularly racy, they did show a presidential candidate committing an inexplicable and foolish lapse of judgment, an act of spectacular self-destruction. Here was a married man who already knew that reporters were preternaturally interested in his sex life. Wearing a T-shirt emblazoned with the words "Monkey Business Crew," he had posed for a photo with a young woman in a miniskirt perched on his knee. That particular photo, along with accompanying pictures inside the tabloid of Hart and Rice enjoying themselves at a nightclub, did not prove he was unfaithful. But it did provide tangible evidence of a public indiscretion.

Unlike the *Herald,* the *Enquirer* had no compunction about paying for photos. By the time the *Enquirer* appeared on the newsstands three weeks after Hart dropped out of the race, almost every newspaper in the country, including the *Miami Herald,* had run a wire service photo of the *Enquirer*'s cover. On the one hand, the *Enquirer* was a "pariah publication,"[30] ostracized by the mainstream for such practices as paying for information. On the other hand, the mainstream freely borrowed stories from the *Enquirer.* David Broder of the *Washington Post,* a dean of political reporters, wrote in 1994 that supermarket tabloids "have demonstrated the capacity to 'launch' stories—often of the sleaziest kind—that the mainstream press feels it necessary to follow."[31]

The view of The Establishment is far from monolithic. Margaret Carlson, then of *Time* magazine, coined the phrase "tabloid laundering," underscoring the hypocrisy of the mainstream press. Carlson's colleague, Dan Goodgame, White House correspondent for *Time,* explained what she meant in a story on the *Enquirer* that appeared in the *Los Angeles Times:* "You let the tabloids go out and pay people for stories and do the dirty things establishment journalists hold themselves above. Then you pick up and cover the controversy, either directly or as a press story. You write: 'Oh, how horrible the press is.' Then you go into the details."[32]

A fan of the *Enquirer* is Sir Harold Evans, former editor of the *Sunday Times* and the *Times* of London, one of the great journalists of the last half of the century. Evans contributed a cover blurb for Iain Calder's book: "Iain Calder never slept with a space alien in his days at the *National Enquirer* (so far as I know), but he found a lot of good stories that had the added advantage of being true, and this book is a splendid romp behind their banner headlines." Ted Koppel, on *Nightline,* once commented that "the paper maintains extremely high journalistic standards."[33]

In its seven decades of covering the bizarre and reporting on high-profile figures, the *National Enquirer* has had its highs and lows. Starting with its coverage of Gary Hart it increasingly became entwined with the establishment press—a symbiosis that culminated in the *Enquirer*'s coverage of the O. J. Simpson case when he was accused of murdering his former wife, Nicole Brown Simpson, and her friend, Ron Goldman.

Unlike the Condit and Hart stories, which the *Enquirer* passed on in their early stages, the Simpson story was vintage *Enquirer* from the start. Ironically, it was not much of a story for others when it first appeared. In the first days after Nicole Simpson and her friend were murdered—their throats cut in a savage attack— the story was relegated to the inside pages of the establishment press, and it received little airtime on network news. But the grisly murders had all the ingredients of a tabloid story. The *Enquirer* flooded the area around Simpson's house with reporters, and it was prepared to pay sources. For the *Enquirer,* money was the great motivator, as it purchased one "exclusive" after another, Calder wrote in his book.[34]

Before the murder trial began, Jose Camacho, a clerk at Ross Cutlery in Los Angeles, initially told reporters that he had not sold a knife to Simpson. Ultimately, Camacho changed his story and admitted to an *Enquirer* reporter that he had indeed sold Simpson a knife, and he produced an autograph that Simpson had signed for him on the day of the purchase. Camacho stated that he saw nothing wrong in profiting from telling the truth. He and the cutlery store owners were paid $12,500 by the *Enquirer.*

This payment created a ruckus. Roger Cossack, a Los Angeles lawyer and a legal analyst, was interviewed by *Nightline,* which, after a slow start, devoted much of its summer to following the aftermath of the Simpson murder case once it became clear that the show's ratings soared when it covered this story. "I mean this is 1994," Cossack said in defense of the *Enquirer*'s payment. "People know that people get paid by the *National Enquirer.* People are poor and understand the need for money. This poor Camacho. He's selling knives for a living, and suddenly here's this situation."[35]

Other supporters of checkbook journalism were quick to point out that people sometimes lie whether they are paid or not. "The important thing is, when you get information, whether you pay for it or not, you check it out, you prove that it's accurate, as much as you can," stated David Perel, the editor at the *Enquirer* in charge of the Simpson coverage, speaking on *Nightline.* "Look at all the information in the so-called mainstream press which was not paid for, but it's been proven to be wholly inaccurate."[36] Arrayed against these arguments were the forces of the mainstream. Howard Kurtz, the media reporter of the *Washington Post,* decried the "journalistic vultures" with "checkbooks in hands."[37] Gilbert Cranberg, the former editor of the *Des Moines Register,* explained: "Mainstream newspapers don't buy news because their editors understand that money paid to a source gives the source motive to invent and embroider; hang a price tag on information and it becomes a commodity."[38]

The issue of checkbook journalism emerged again in the Simpson story at the end of 1995—just before the start of the trial—and this time around, the *Enquirer* had a most unlikely ally: a *New York*

Times reporter. David Margolick, who covered the pretrial maneuverings and the trial itself for the *Times,* twice cited an *Enquirer* story in which it had been reported that Simpson had been overheard yelling, "I did it," during a confessional jailhouse meeting with his minister and friend, the former professional football star Roosevelt Grier. Margolick's citation came at a point where he described a court hearing concerning whether a sheriff's deputy would be allowed to testify at trial about overhearing remarks that Simpson may have made to Grier. At the hearing, the deputy told of listening from an adjoining room to Simpson speaking in a raised voice. Because of the minister-penitent legal privilege, Grier was not permitted to testify about this conversation, which meant the jury would never hear about it unless the deputy's testimony was allowed.

Yet millions of Americans knew about it—from the *National Enquirer* and from the *New York Times.* "The only published account of the conversation appears in this week's *National Enquirer,*"[39] Margolick wrote. "Attributing its report to an unnamed jail guard, it said that Mr. Grier told Mr. Simpson, who held a Bible at the time, that he could not expect mercy and salvation unless he was honest with God and admitted his failings. At that point, the guard told the publication, Mr. Simpson exclaimed: 'I did it.'" Then, less than a week later, Margolick repeated essentially the same version of the story.[40] Margolick's story attracted attention: it was one of the first times a mainstream paper had acknowledged the *Enquirer* approvingly.

Margolick later told the *Washington Post:* "It was from a source that had proven itself reliable in the Simpson case, and I'd be doing my readers a disservice if I didn't mention it."[41] Margolick repeated the same rationale on the *Today* show, arguing that to have ignored the *Enquirer*'s report would have made his article inexplicable to readers. He repeated his contention that the *Enquirer* was more reliable than *Time* magazine or the *New Yorker* in its coverage of the Simpson story. What Margolick did not mention was that in addition to its "record of accuracy," the *Enquirer* employed techniques—such as paying sources—that no establishment publication would use directly.

The *Times* was skewered for attributing its information to an unnamed source in a supermarket tabloid that often paid for information. A less-than-happy Joseph Lelyveld, the executive editor of the *Times,* was quoted in his own paper reminding readers that the *Times* was not "subcontracting our editorial judgment in the Simpson case to a supermarket tabloid."[42] The *Enquirer* relished its newly won respectability, ultimately taking out a full-page advertisement in the *New York Times* to brag about its well-known admirers,[43] and ten years later, editors at the *Enquirer* still referred to Margolick's praise of the tabloid as a high watermark in the publication's history.

It seems to me that news outlets need to get beyond their discomfort with paying *any* sources for *anything*. A quarter of a century ago, Donald Trelford, editor of the *Observer* in London, a man who came from the English tradition, where payments are sometimes acceptable, put it succinctly: "People who possess information are entitled to sell it."[44] It did not seem to Trelford—or to an articulate minority—that payment is unethical if that is the only way to secure important information. In defense of checkbook journalism, shortly before the Simpson murders John Tierney, a libertarian on the staff of the *New York Times,* wrote:

> Many people allow themselves to be quoted because they want publicity for selfish reasons: winning votes, impressing clients and colleagues, pushing an agenda, selling books, albums, tickets,

stock shares, gadgets. They have essentially arranged for someone else to pay them for being in the paper. I don't believe that paying sources is unethical, as long as it's disclosed to the reader; in some cases I think it makes for better journalism. It gives a share of the profits to sources who spend time and take risks. It might promote some fictional tales, but it would also elicit stories that otherwise wouldn't be told from the many people who now see no good reason to talk to a reporter.[45]

Journalism organizations themselves freely pay for consultants and those providing an inside look at government. In fields other than journalism, people pay for quality information. One wants the most knowledgeable stockbroker, the smartest lawyer. The act of receiving payment in exchange for information is embedded in the criminal justice system. Every day, suspected and convicted criminals are offered compensation in the form of reduced sentences in exchange for their testimony. Informants are often directly paid money by government agents for information. That information, of course, is subject to scrutiny. Paid sources may have an incentive not to tell the truth. But this does not seem terribly different from what is already the case: sources who are not paid may also have an incentive not to tell the truth.

Absolute prohibitions against checkbook journalism, particularly in a globalized age, seem quaint and probably do not work anyway. Michael Wines of the *Times* wrote movingly from Africa in 2006 of the complexity of paying for information particularly in poor parts of the world: "In reputable journalism, paying for information is a cardinal sin, the notion being that a source who will talk only for money is to say anything to earn his payment." He explained his rule for paying sources: he never pays in advance of an interview. He does what he can, though. He described his joy in paying for food for sources who lived outside of Lusaka, the capital of Zambia: "They are stone-crushers, a class of laborers who cling to the lowest social rung even in this, one of the world's poorest nations. Their lives are as miserable as those of almost any group I have seen in three years in Africa." After a few hours of interviews with these laborers about their struggle to survive, Wines drove to a grocery store and bought $75 worth of food—cornmeal, cooking oil, rice, orange concentrate, bread, milk, candy. "I returned and unloaded it to undiluted pandemonium—mothers' riotous joy; youngsters mobbing for sweets; actual dancing in the street for 30 people, a real live Christmas in July."[46]

Wines engaged in checkbook journalism from altruistic, humanitarian instincts, which are far different from the motives of tabloids like the *National Enquirer* in paying grizzled informants. But there are fundamental, underlying similarities between what Wines did and what the tabloids do—a journalist is exchanging something of value (access or space or, in much rarer instances, money) for information. This kind of exchange is at the heart of most journalistic transactions. People do not ordinarily speak to journalists out of high-mindedness. They want something in return—to see their name in headlines, to get their point of view across, or, in the case of checkbook journalism, to receive tangible consideration.

SEVEN

MISADVENTURES IN
FACT-CHECKING

It is a rare piece of journalism that cannot after publication be made to look slipshod, and so I begin this chapter with an illustration of an obituary that turned out to be just that. It is discomfiting to relate this anecdote, as it is partially about me and involves the obituary of a former colleague who died in 2006. The example illustrates the challenge of finding journalistic truth, a challenge that engaged Jim Carey, an icon in his field and probably the leading communications theorist of his generation, who died on May 23, 2006.[1] The *New York Times* obituary had the date of his death wrong. It mistakenly recorded the date Carey left as dean of the College of Communications at the University of Illinois to become a professor at Columbia University Graduate School of Journalism. The obituary also misstated the length of the more academically rigorous master's degree program that he helped to develop at Columbia. It is one year, not two. The obituary is almost a textbook example of what Jay Matthews, a veteran reporter, wrote years earlier: "how narrowly the correctable mistake is defined and how many errors never get corrected."[2]

The paper did publish corrections for some of those mistakes within a few days. But more problematic than the narrow factual errors in the Carey obituary, at least for me (and perhaps only me), were the errors that did not get corrected. A section of the obituary dealt with Jim's unsuccessful effort to become dean at

Columbia in 1996, a subject of keen interest to me. In the obituary, James Boylan, who had published his labor of love, a history of the school, *Pulitzer's School: Columbia University's School of Journalism, 1903–2003,* is paraphrased as writing that Carey was rejected as dean "after journalism practitioners demanded one of their own." That is not quite what the book said. Boylan had written that Carey became aware of opposition "when the search committee heard from graduates urging the appointment of a practitioner."[3]

I was the person who was chosen as dean instead of Carey, and the account in the obituary is not at all the way I remember what happened. In early 1996 Jim Carey had said on two occasions to the provost that he did not wish to be considered for the job. To ensure that he was insulated from consideration, he told friends and colleagues, including me, that he had accepted a position on the search committee for the dean. Only at the last minute, deep into the search process, did he decide to become a candidate, then stepping down from the search committee.

At this time, I had just left my job as dean at Berkeley after spending eight years there and was happily enjoying a sabbatical, with no thought or desire of ever being a dean again. One afternoon I was contacted by Jonathan Cole, the Columbia provost, whom I had never met or spoken to. In the course of an hour-long conversation, he persuaded me to apply for the job, suggesting that, given my experience, I stood an excellent chance of getting it.

It was Cole, not the search committee, who appointed the dean. He chose me, Cole later told me, because I had previous experience *as a dean*—at a school similar to Columbia—not, as the *Times* obituary suggested, because I had been a working journalist. I had been a reporter, but that was years earlier. Neither Jonathan Cole nor I was interviewed by the *Times* to corroborate or illuminate the facts in the obituary. Several disclosures are necessary here. I commissioned the book by Jim Boylan, an old friend and a former teacher of mine, shortly after I was named dean. He interviewed me a couple of times, and not, as I recall, about this topic. Jim Boylan and Jim Carey had been close friends for years, and in the book Boylan does acknowledge that his version of events came from Carey.

I understand, of course, that there may be a different truth from the one that I remember or the one that Jonathan Cole remembers. Jim Carey may have *thought* he lost the deanship because practitioners interceded, and he may have related this to others. Jim Boylan may have had the same suspicions. Many of his admirers certainly would have wanted and expected Carey to be named dean. Jim Carey was an exceptional scholar and a remarkable, if sometimes prickly, man. I had known him for many years before I came to Columbia, and I specifically told Jonathan Cole when he recruited me that I thought Jim should be named dean. But that did not happen. After I was named, Jim was not pleased with Columbia or with me, but he stayed on as a professor. Our relationship soured.

An added poignancy to all this occurred when, after Jim's death, a 1991 interview with him was posted on a Columbia website. "There are no final thoughts," he said. He continued:

> I quote all the time these wonderful lines of Kenneth Burke [the philosopher]. Life is a conversation. When we enter, it is already going on. We try to catch the drift of it. We exit before it's over. The first lesson any pragmatist learns is that at the hour of our death, we are rewriting our biography for the last time. And then the first hour into our death, someone else rewrites the biography for us. Our children, our spouses, our friends. Do you remember

what he was like . . . what he said . . . what he did . . . And so in that sense, life is a conversation that continuously goes on, that continuously renews itself, and, therefore, renews you. All work is a matter of self-renewal, which is a renewal of the other. No one has the last word. There are no final thoughts, there is no end to the conversation.[4]

On a more prosaic level, why was the *Times* story not checked out more closely? The simple answer is that newspapers typically do not check facts. Nor, for that matter, are books like Boylan's routinely fact-checked. It would be an expensive, often unwieldy process, and there is no legal obligation to do so. In a groundbreaking opinion on privacy rights, Justice William Brennan in 1967 sided with the old *Life* magazine, which had created a false impression in a photo essay that a play, *The Desperate Hours,* had depicted the reenactment of an experience of the Hill family, which had been held hostage in their home near Philadelphia. In the play, the family was brutally beaten up; in reality, those who held the Hills hostage had done them no harm. The Hill family could not be awarded damages, Justice Brennan ruled in *Time v. Hill,* for false reports of matters of public interest in the absence of proof that the report was published with knowledge of its falsity or in reckless disregard of the truth. Brennan continued: "We create a grave risk of serious impairment of the indispensable service of a free press in a free society if we saddle the press with the impossible burden of verifying to a certainty the facts associated in news articles with a person's name, picture or portrait."[5] No opinion since then has altered this holding.

Even without a legal obligation, over the past decade or so many news organizations, faced with a crisis of credibility, have increased the frequency of their corrections. But by no means is every error corrected. Naturally, someone first has to spot the error, and someone then has to complain. For numerous reasons, these two conditions are often not met, and readers are never informed that the errors are made. For instance, no correction resulted from a series of stories in the *Times* on May 31, 2006, reporting that President Bush had named Henry Paulson, the head of Goldman Sachs, as the new secretary of the treasury. In the very detailed suite of stories that appeared in the *Times* that day, it was noted that Paulson had been offered the job on May 21, ten days earlier. Bush had hidden this fact from reporters. But reporters became all-too-willing accomplices in obscuring the truth. On May 27, in a front-page story, the *Times* reported: "President Bush is leaning toward having one of his oldest friends take over the Treasury Department after a fruitless effort thus far to woo a star from Wall Street. Republicans with close ties to the White House said on Friday that Donald Evans, the former commerce secretary and a longtime Texas friend of the president, was a leading contender to succeed John Snow who has indicated his desire to step down by early July."[6]

The problem is clear: the speculative story on Saturday, May 27, was just not true. A decision to name somebody else—a bona fide Wall Street star—had already been made, if not yet announced. The story was not true in ways that journalism has been slow to grasp. The administration willfully misled reporters in order to preserve a secret. But the reader was not let in on this even after reporters knew because in the *New York Times*'s blanket coverage of Paulson's appointment on May 31, the name of Donald Evans, who had been the front-runner four days before, was nowhere to be found. Crucial context was missing. Admission of faulty earlier reporting was absent. Presumably, no one had complained.

Had there been a layer of fact-checking at the newspaper, this error might have been avoided. "Fact-checking," a term often used imprecisely to define a multitude of activities, must be distinguished from the type of prepublication review of the *National Enquirer* that the tabloid's lawyers conducted, starting in the 1980s. Lawyers typically flag only legally actionable portions of copy. They are not supposed to guarantee factual accuracy. Classic fact-checking occurs late in the editorial process, just before publication, where a staff member or contract employee is assigned to confirm independently every "fact" in an author's draft. For instance, if a fact-checker had been assigned to confirm the year Carey arrived at Columbia, that person would have contacted the University of Illinois, where he came from, or looked at documentation from Columbia to know when he arrived. Instead, I surmise, the author relied on a passage in Boylan's book, which said: "Among the newer faculty, two stood out. " The first of these stand-outs arrived in 1988. "The other major addition," Boylan wrote, "was James W. Carey."[7] Boylan does not give a specific year for Carey's arrival, and the author of the obituary apparently inferred—erroneously, as it turned out—that Jim also arrived in 1988.

Fact-checking is a distant luxury in daily newsrooms, where reporters must be their own fact-checkers.[8] Formal fact-checking is more common in magazines than anyplace else. But there can be a maddening literal-mindedness to fact-checking even at the finest magazines, according to Richard Blow and Ari Posner, who wrote an article in the *New Republic* entitled "Adventures in Fact Checking: Are You Completely Bald?" (The handful of articles written about fact-checking, it should be noted, share a striking characteristic: they have cute, even clever, headlines that tend to underscore the narrowness of the process.) Blow and Posner wrote this article in the late 1980s after the culture of fact-checking had gotten a big boost, or at least a lot of publicity, from *Bright Lights, Big City,* Jay McInerney's novel that chronicled the tribulations of an aspiring writer disillusioned with his job as a fact-checker at a magazine resembling the *New Yorker.* For Blow and Posner, the theory of fact-checking is "that even the tiniest details are part of a larger whole, like bricks in a building."[9]

But fact-checking as practiced, while surely better than doing nothing, has its limitations. Even if every quote may be "accurate," the research department can only confirm that the "fact" in question was said by someone. Researchers cannot discover what sources may have said that was omitted, other facts that were left out, or what sources who were not consulted would have said. Nor can they determine what the context was.[10] In a monograph, "This Paper Has Not Been Fact Checked," the author Susan Shapiro distinguished between the "checkable" fact—a person's name and title, the spelling of a proper noun, the geographic location of events, the color of a shirt, the date of a historical event, and so forth—and more subtle questions, such as whether the evidence is credible and whether it supports the conclusions drawn from them.[11]

In a column entitled "What Do You Know, and How Do You Know It?" Daniel Okrent, who brought extensive experience in magazine editing to his job as the first public editor of the *New York Times,* had this to say about the distinction between how newspapers and magazines treat fact-checking: "Newspaper reporters aspire to corroboration of disputed facts by relying on more than one source," while magazines "do the same, but they may not provide the evidence in print."[12]

In an astute observation, Okrent underscored the limitations of fact-checking: "At magazines, fact-checking can help you get details right, but can't pin down the un-pindownable: sometimes, a source will make an assertion—for instance, that he saw women walking through Cottonwood, Calif. in high heels. . . . Virtually all the fact-checker can do is call the source and ask: 'Did you see women walking through Cottonwood Canyon in high heels?' The firmest 'yes' doesn't even approach proof. It is often not the fact that gets checked, but the fact that someone said it was a fact." So, in a sense, fact-checkers may be less champions of truth "than followers of ritualistic methodological routines."[13]

A marvelous essay from what is now another generation, "There Are oo Trees in Russia: The Function of Facts in Newsmagazines," appeared in *Harper's Magazine* more than forty years ago. It was written by Otto Friedrich, a prolific, mordant, and wise magazine writer and author who was disenchanted with much of twentieth-century culture. "That men should live at peace with one another might be described as the truth, but it is not a fact, nor is it news," he wrote. "That a certain number of children were born yesterday in Chicago is a fact, and the truth, but not news. Journalism involves an effort to discover, select, and assemble certain facts in a way that will be not only reasonably true but reasonably interesting—and therefore reasonably salable."[14]

Friedrich specified a truism of journalism as he speculated about why we are sometimes inundated with minutiae. Journalism is based, he said, "on the theory that knowledge of lesser facts implies knowledge of major facts."[15] He recalled how, on one occasion, a newsmagazine editor wrote into a piece of copy: "There are oo trees in Russia," expecting the fact-checker to research and fill in an appropriate figure. The fact-checker, he wrote, "took a creative delight in such an impossible problem. From the Soviet government she ascertained the number of acres officially listed as forests; from some Washington agency she ascertained the average number of trees per acre of forests. The result was a wholly improbable but wholly unchallengeable statistic for the number of trees in Russia."[16]

In another example, Friedrich punctured the characteristically American desire for certainty and aversion to ambiguity and nuance. He recalled that during one of the periodic mid-century crises in Laos, an American correspondent bitterly complained to a Laotian government spokesman that he had spoken to sixteen government officials and gotten sixteen different versions of the facts. "The Laotian was bewildered," Friedrich wrote. "It seemed perfectly natural to him, he said, that if you spoke to sixteen different officials you would get sixteen different answers." For Friedrich, "the Laotian was wise in acknowledging and answering the first fundamental question about the fetish of facts: Does it really matter which 'fact' is to be officially certified as 'true'? He was equally wise in acknowledging and answering a second question: Does anyone really know which 'fact' is 'true'? He was equally wise in raising a third question, and implying an answer: Every man sees the 'facts' according to his own interests."[17]

No wonder that even magazines with the largest and most skilled fact-checking departments have not devised foolproof systems. Though many techniques of ensuring accuracy remain—at *Business Week,* it has been called "red dotting," and at other magazines, green, black, or red pencils are used to denote the items to be double-checked—it is becoming harder to find full-fledged fact-checking departments or even full-time fact-checkers. Actually, most weekly and bimonthly magazines long ago abandoned the term "fact-checker" as an archaic job title.[18] Checkers at the *New Republic,* which has published as many articles on the art of fact-checking as any other publication, were deceived by a young, rising star reporter, Stephen Glass, who fabricated hundreds of facts, quotations, individuals, and events and constructed elaborate ruses to escape detection by fact-checkers. These misadventures were transformed into *The Fabulist,* Glass's novel, and an excellent movie called *Shattered Glass.*

The *New Yorker* has viewed itself as the gold standard of fact-checking. A booklet on fact-checking that it formerly distributed began simply: "You can trust what you read in the *New Yorker.*"[19] The magazine tries to make sure that, as far as possible, every word in every piece has been verified independently. But that is a standard impossible to meet. Many inaccuracies have occurred at the *New Yorker* along the way, the perpetrators belonging to the pantheon of the great *New Yorker* writers.

Oddly, the predominant theme of the problematic articles is food and drink, not affairs of state or finance or love. Joseph Mitchell used a composite so that his stories set in the Fulton Fish Market would be "truthful rather than factual." Alastair Reid re-created a flyblown bar in Barcelona that had long ago closed. In a profile, John McPhee's unnamed protagonist accused Lutece, the famed New York restaurant, of selling frozen turbot as fresh. The marathon libel case that former Freud scholar Jeffrey Masson brought against the *New Yorker*'s Janet Malcolm was based in part on whether an interview took place over baked goat cheese at Chez Panisse in Berkeley, California, or over breakfast at Malcolm's Manhattan home.

In 1944 and 1945, the *New Yorker* ran three articles on a ninety-three-year-old Fulton Fish Market peddler named Hugh G. Flood, who "often tells people that he is dead set and determined to live until the afternoon of July 27, 1965, when he will be 115 years old. 'I don't ask much here below,' he says. 'I just want to hit a 115. That'll hold me.'"[20] Unbeknownst to the dozens of readers who tried to get in touch with Mr. Flood, there never was a Hugh G. Flood. He had been invented by the article's author, Joseph Mitchell, one of the great writers of the mid-century. Mitchell admitted as much three years later, in 1948, when he published the articles as a book. Mitchell apparently felt that the facts would have gotten in the way of the truth. In the preface to his book, he wrote: "Mr. Flood is not one man; combined in him are aspects of several old men who work or hang out in Fulton Fish Market, or who did in the past. I wanted these stories to be truthful rather than factual, but they are solidly based on facts."[21]

Alastair Reid, another venerated *New Yorker* writer, in a "Letter from Barcelona," described Spaniards sitting in "a small, flyblown bar"[22] in that city openly jeering at a television speech being given by the Spanish dictator, Francisco Franco. In fact, the bar no longer existed. Reid had watched Franco's speech in the home of the tavern's onetime bartender. So legendary is the *New Yorker*'s concern for accuracy that its failure to adhere to its own high standards becomes news. The fictional scene and several other deceptions that Reid admitted to were disclosed many years later in a page-one story of the *Wall Street Journal*.[23] That was followed the next day by a front-page story in the *New York Times* and by major stories in other publications across the country.

In Reid's own mind, however, he had done nothing wrong, and he felt the controversy was silly. "In reporting with some accuracy, at times we have to go much further than the strictly factual," he said. "Facts are part of the perceived whole."[24] The article that had attracted the attention had been published in December 1961, and the bar had been closed for years before then. No one was harmed. No one would have remembered anyhow after a few days whether such jeering took place or not.

The author of the *Wall Street Journal* story had been a student in the Yale seminar where Reid had openly discussed his techniques.

Soon after the seminar was over, she joined the *Journal,* and she wrote the story after having interviewed Reid. The ground rules of the seminar were ambiguous, but there would have been no 1984 story had Reid not volunteered reminiscences in 1983 of that 1961 article.[25] A longtime *New Yorker* staff writer supported Reid in the *Journal* article, saying it was permissible to change facts in nonfiction articles as long as they were faithful to a "larger reality." E. J. Kahn, another *New Yorker* writer, told the *New York Times,* "If you're having a conversation with somebody on an airplane and you want to make it a train because it's better for the piece, I don't see that it's all that dreadful." Although Reid was initially supported by the legendary editor of the *New Yorker,* William Shawn, in a subsequent memorandum, Shawn wrote that Reid had made a "journalistic mistake." The editors of the *New Yorker* "do not condone what he did."[26]

John McPhee, the meticulous and prolific author, devoted a twenty-five-thousand-word profile in a February 1979 issue of the *New Yorker* to the world's most perfect country restaurant. So perfect was the restaurant that McPhee would not divulge the location, lest it be spoiled. But he teased readers by divulging its distance from New York City and the travel time. Without naming the man, McPhee quoted the judgment of the chef and owner about "some of the loftiest meccas of gastronomy, some of which he 'guessed' were serving frozen ingredients, most especially the turbot and Dover sole at Lutece."[27] In her memoir, *Eating My Words: An Appetite for Life,* partly a recollection of her days as restaurant reviewer at the *New York Times,* Mimi Sheraton tells how she and her colleague Frank Prial unmasked the identity of the secret restaurant and found that McPhee had exaggerated its brilliance.

In mock high dudgeon, *Time* magazine reported that the accusation about the frozen turbot "stirred temblors in Manhattan stockpots." Lutece's chef Andre Soltner indignantly produced fish-market receipts to show that his turbot was fresh. The accuser apologized, and the usually meticulous *New Yorker* explained that in deference to McPhee its rules of fact-checking had been suspended in order to preserve the anonymity of the quoted restaurant owner. According to *Time,* "it had taken the exceptional step of allowing the author of the piece to do most of the checking on his own," depriving Soltner of a chance to refute the claims before the article appeared.[28]

Finally, the need for meticulous checking was reinforced by a prolonged lawsuit against the writer Janet Malcolm, who ultimately admitted reconstructing lengthy quotes in a *New Yorker* profile published in 1983 of Jeffrey M. Masson, a Sanskrit scholar turned psychoanalyst. In the late 1970s, Masson had met Dr. Kurt Eissler, then head of the Sigmund Freud Archives in London, and Freud's daughter, Anna Freud. Masson was soon hired to be projects director of the Sigmund Freud Archives. Within a year, he was fired from that position after giving a lecture at Yale in which he questioned Freud's theory of child sexual abuse and indirectly blamed Freud for "the present-day sterility of psychoanalysis throughout the world."[29] To the dismay of the Freudian establishment, Masson had suggested that the "seduction theory" attributing adult neurosis to childhood sexual abuse may have been right after all, but that Freud may have abandoned it for personal as much as for scientific reasons. In an interview, the garrulous and provocative Masson claimed that his findings would drastically alter psychotherapy. "They would have to recall every patient since 1901," he said. "It would be like the Pinto."[30]

Masson, an engaging fellow with a penchant for talking and talking, made fine material for a profile, and in 1983 Malcolm published a forty-five-thousand-word, two-part profile in the *New*

Yorker. Masson, who was called by a checker during the fact-checking process, claimed that he was concerned about factual inaccuracies and asked to see portions of the article that referred to him, but that did not happen. (The researcher involved disputed that version of the telephone conversation.)[31] At the time he sued Malcolm, the magazine, and the book publisher in 1984, Masson was running a sandwich shop in Berkeley. I met him shortly after that. He stopped by my office in Berkeley one day, unannounced, to ask me about the rules of the appropriate use of quotations. We became friends.

In his lawsuit, he claimed that Malcolm had fabricated many of the statements attributed to him in order to portray him in a false and defamatory fashion. A lower-court judge threw out the case, on a summary judgment motion, explaining that Malcolm's language was a "rational interpretation" of Masson's tape-recorded statements. The appeal languished for years—until Janet Malcolm caused an uproar among journalists when she published articles that became *The Journalist and the Murderer* (which I examine in the next chapter). Outside interest in the result of the appeal grew, and the U.S. Court of Appeals for the Ninth Circuit, by a 2–1 vote, affirmed the dismissal. But in a lengthy, well-researched dissent, which he later described to me as a "deep dissent," Judge Alex Kozinski, who delighted in being known as provocateur, criticized Malcolm and her publishers: "Truth is a journalist's stock in trade. To invoke the right to deliberately distort what someone else has said is to assert the right to lie in print."[32]

Based on the strength of this dissent, Judge Kozinski's friend, Justice Antonin Scalia of the U.S. Supreme Court, urged that the high court hear the case. Adopting the rationale of Kozinski's dissent, the Supreme Court decided that the primary issue before it was whether the attributed quotations had the degree of falsity required to prove that Malcolm knew the untruth of what she was attributing to Masson and that it would injure his reputation. The Court found that five quotations in dispute varied sufficiently from the words on Malcolm's tapes that a jury could find that Malcolm knew that what she was attributing to Masson was untrue.

Therefore, the Court concluded that Janet Malcolm would have to endure a jury trial, which would decide whether she deliberately falsified statements that she attributed to Masson. The question for the jury to decide became whether the quotations she attributed to Masson had been fabricated or were just rearranged and compressed. Malcolm argued that she was more than a court stenographer. She just wanted to produce a coherent account for her readers. At the first trial, the jury concluded that Malcolm had fabricated the five statements attributed to Masson and that he had been libeled by two of them. However, the jury deadlocked on damages, and a second trial was held. The second jury found that Malcolm had erred, but it cleared her of legal responsibility. The jury ruled that two of the five disputed quotations that Malcolm had attributed to Masson were false, but that she had not written them with the recklessness that would have been necessary for him to recover damages for libel.[33]

The inescapable conclusion from all these examples is that even the best writers make mistakes—or take unacceptable liberties— and that the best fact-checkers in the world cannot stop them. Although no one has quantified the extent of the problem, it may be worse than the average reader would expect. Newspapers, magazines, and books are the main sources that fact-checkers use to confirm the facts they approve for publication. But books may be even less authoritative than newspapers or magazines, for the standards of evidence required of book authors can be quite weak. Fact-checking is not generally considered part of the book-publishing process, and publishers do not guarantee the accuracy of books they publish.

This calls into question the widely held assumption that hardbound volumes "are society's most reliable record,"[34] the "vessels traditionally used to convey patient reflection into the archives."[35] Publishers accept, on faith, the assertion of an author, and this understanding is embedded in book contracts, which ordinarily require an author to warrant that the facts are true or are based on reasonable research. The proper analogy for the book industry, publishers argue, is not the newspaper or magazine article, but the signed column—a blend of fact and opinion aimed at promoting a particular point of view.[36] Opinions, after all, can never be wrong. "A belief or a conviction, no matter how illogical, crackbrained or infuriating, is an idea subject to vigorous dispute but is not an assertion subject to editorial or legal correction," William Safire, who was paid for more than thirty years to have opinions for the *New York Times,* e-mailed to a *Times* colleague.[37]

When Adam Cohen, of the *New York Times* editorial board, was a reporter for *Time* magazine, he and Richard Lacayo deftly picked apart Philip Howard's *The Death of Common Sense: How Law Is Suffocating America,* the 1995 best-selling book that attacked the American legal system. Years later, Cohen recalled how he was asked to check out some of the anecdotes, and he was "shocked by how poorly they held up."[38] For instance, when Howard complained about the costs imposed by the federal Americans with Disabilities Act, enacted in 1990, he cited Minnetonka, Minnesota, where city officials "had to alter the municipal hockey rink to make the scorer's box wheelchair accessible."[39] "When was that?" asked Kathy Magrew, the city official who had monitored compliance with the act.

In Magrew's account, according to Lacayo and Cohen, when

Minnetonka was asked to develop plans to accommodate disabled people who might want to keep score, officials submitted estimates on the cost of altering the box, but they also determined that the disability law could be met simply by moving the scorer's equipment out of the box whenever a disabled person asked them to. When Magrew was interviewed by the team from *Time,* she said that no one had asked her about this. "You have to use common sense," she playfully told the reporters. Howard's book is full of anecdotes about silly rules and harebrained regulations. As the team from *Time* concluded, "The problem with trial by anecdote, however, is that it can play rough with the rules of evidence. On closer examination some of Howard's best tales turn out to be more complicated than they seem in his brisk retellings."[40]

In 2002, Howard, by then a senior corporate strategist with Covington and Burling, the distinguished Washington-based law firm, founded Common Good, a national bipartisan coalition organized to restore common sense to American law. At the time that *Time* magazine rained on his best-seller's parade, Howard put much of the blame on a researcher who had helped him with the book.[41] A decent fact-checker would have saved Howard much embarrassment. Somehow, the justifications against using fact-checkers—they are too expensive, too cumbersome, too slow—ring hollow. It strikes me that fact-checking is not a luxury, but a necessity, particularly for the many stories in the daily press that are not breaking news, but prepared over a period of days or weeks—certainly sufficient time for a fact-checker to review them.

Over the past decade, the trend at many magazines has been away from fact-checking, with cost cited as the reason. Increasingly at these publications, the journalist is now responsible for the accuracy of the article. In a setting where stories have long lead times, either in newspapers, magazines, or books, some sort of independent fact-checking seems to be called for. Those publications facing tighter deadlines might borrow from a policy promulgated in 2006 by the Bloomberg News Service. I know of the policy because I have been a consultant to Bloomberg. I had nothing at all to do with its formulation. The policy states:

> Reporters should check the accuracy of all facts, including names of people, companies, organizations and locations. They should also check all ages (including birth dates). . . .
>
> For quotes, reporters must check that the comment is accurate, that it was said by the person it's attributed to, and that the quote is in context. . . .
>
> Emphasis is placed on eyewitness observation.
>
> Wherever possible, physical descriptions of people, places and events should be based on what reporters see with their own eyes and hear with their own ears, buttressed by information from authoritative sources about details like height, weight, width, capacity, temperature and distance. . . .
>
> Echoing lessons taught in elementary school and high school, the policy places a premium on using primary sources. Primary sources include interviews conducted by the reporter who wrote the story; official documents such as financial reports, transcripts of legal proceedings, public meetings and press conferences, and company and organization Web sites. . . .
>
> Reporters should always strive to get information from primary sources. Somebody else's story, including a previously published Bloomberg News story, is not a primary source.
>
> Facts change. Prices rise and fall. People get older and move to new jobs. Companies go public or go private or get taken over. Even countries can change names. That's why every fact has to be checked—every time a reporter writes a story.[42]

With its emphasis on meticulous checking, eyewitness observation, and use of primary sources, this policy could serve as a useful starting point for other news organizations and publishers. Other daily news organizations have taken a different approach to fact-checking. During the 2004 presidential race, many news organizations fact-checked the claims of the candidates during the campaign, including points they made in their debates and advertisements. Rather than merely repeating what politicians said, journalists checked the underlying validity of claims and assertions, and when they found discrepancies, they published their findings.

An independent fact-checking organization, FactCheck.org, was established at the Annenberg Public Policy Center of the University of Pennsylvania. Its director, Brooks Jackson, is a former reporter for the Associated Press, the *Wall Street Journal,* and CNN, where, starting in the 1992 presidential election, he produced "ad watch" and "fact check" stories to disclose misleading political statements.

"We monitor the factual accuracy of what is said by major U.S. political players in the form of TV ads, debates, speeches, interviews, and news releases," states the website of FactCheck.org.[43] "Our goal is to apply the best practices of both journalism and scholarship, and to increase public knowledge and understanding." The slogan of the site is the famous, if slightly ungrammatical, aphorism from the late New York Senator Daniel P. Moynihan: "Everyone is entitled to their own opinion, but not their own facts."

EIGHT

JANET MALCOLM'S
SPECIAL TRUTHS

Truth, Janet Malcolm wrote in her most recent book, *The Crime of Sheila McGough*, is "messy, incoherent, aimless, boring, absurd."[1] Truth is surely all these things and much more in the collected writings of Malcolm. She is the daughter of a psychiatrist steeped in Freud, started as a photography critic, and has explored different ways of knowing: from psychoanalysis to journalism to biography to legal proceedings. In *The Crime of Sheila McGough*, as in one of her earlier books, *The Journalist and the Murderer*, Malcolm used a legal proceeding to raise important questions about the capacity of both law and journalism to find truth. Though it is easy to argue against her answers to the enduring question, "What is truth?"—as I show in this chapter—her reasoning is worth looking at in detail, as a case study of sorts, to gain a greater understanding of the complex web that truth can weave, and the difficulty that the journalist confronts in the attempt to unravel it.

In the highly successful earlier book, she came very close to exonerating her protagonist, Jeffrey MacDonald, who had been accused of murdering his wife and children in 1970, but she stopped just short of concluding that MacDonald had been unfairly convicted. In her later book, however, she decided that Sheila McGough, a criminal defense lawyer, was in fact framed and had been wrongly convicted of fraud, perjury, and witness intimidation in Alexandria, Virginia. In one of her signature sweeping statements, Malcolm wrote that "trials are won by attorneys whose stories fit, and lost by those whose stories are like the shapeless housecoat that truth, in her disdain for appearances, has chosen as her uniform." (In a review of the book, Richard A. Posner, a federal appeals judge, concluded that this quote and other "anti-law cracks" describe "her own technique better than it does the law."[2])

So these are the major themes of Malcolm's works: the limited means, whether by legal proceeding, psychiatry, journalism, or biography, that we have at our disposal for finding truth. In much of her writing, in fact, particularly in *The Journalist and the Murderer,* she reflects, directly or indirectly, on her own journalistic techniques and how she must fall short of capturing truth. She is looking at herself within a hall of mirrors.

The Journalist and the Murderer, which began as two magazine articles in the *New Yorker* and an essay in the *New York Review of Books,* was judged as one of the top one hundred nonfiction books of the twentieth century written in English, as selected by a panel of the Modern Library.[3] It caused a sensation when it was published. MacDonald was a former army surgeon and Green Beret captain, and when he was convicted of stabbing and bludgeoning his wife and two young daughters to death in their Fort Bragg, North Carolina, home, the case received ample attention in the press. He was written about in newspapers and magazines as well as in Joe McGinniss's best-selling book *Fatal Vision,* which was adapted as a television movie. His case was reviewed in nearly a score of judicial opinions. MacDonald, in his defense, claimed that the real killers were drug-crazed hippies who chanted: "Acid is groovy, kill the pigs." But it was McGinniss's book that attracted Malcolm's attention, because it became the subject of a lawsuit in 1984. MacDonald brought the case because he felt betrayed by

McGinniss, who had arranged to observe MacDonald throughout the trial in order to conduct research for his book. MacDonald had assumed he would be portrayed sympathetically in the book, but this did not turn out to be the case.

Malcolm, in turn, analyzed McGinniss's relationship with MacDonald in *The Journalist and the Murderer*. In the end, *The Journalist and the Murderer* can be read on many levels: Malcolm's arresting first paragraph, that a journalist "is a kind of confidence man, preying on people's vanity, ignorance, or loneliness." Her view that journalism, at its core, is "morally indefensible." Her disdain of workaday journalists, and her penchant for telling stories on herself, since after all, she too is a journalist. Her unorthodox technique of exhuming a trial after it has ended. Her positioning herself, with no fresh reporting but with plenty of insights, as the arbiter of whether a man actually committed the murders of which he was convicted. Her pointed omission of any discussion of Jeffrey Masson, the exuberant ex-psychoanalyst she had once profiled, even though her legal predicament involving Masson in ways mirrored the story she was telling.

Malcolm's world is a place where people talk,[4] and in that world, many people say they are trying to find the truth—so many people, in fact, that the very idea of truth slips away in the noise. She is a lovely but inconsistent writer, capable of withering insights on one page and pretentious incoherence on the next. She is both elegant and outrageous. Seized by a need for hyperbole, she litters the pages of her work with goofy generalizations: all journalists are conmen; biographers are voyeurs; people who have never sued anyone or been sued have missed a "narcissistic pleasure" unlike any other; all of us have committed murder in our conscious and unconscious imaginations. Playing footsy with her audience, she harshly judges others while she may—or may not—be reflecting on her own predicament in a hip, postmodern way.

Things are just not what they seem. She concludes without equivocation that Joe McGinniss did betray his subject. MacDonald, who never wavered from his not-guilty plea, entered into a formal agreement with McGinniss, who had written *The Selling of the President 1968* and other books. The arrangement gave McGinniss special access to MacDonald and his legal team—McGinniss even lived with MacDonald during the murder trial. In return, MacDonald received a percentage of the book's profits, allowing him to raise money for his legal defense. On another level, it gave MacDonald an insurance policy. If the actual trial went badly (as it did), McGinniss's book could serve as a people's court of appeals, showing the world that MacDonald was not guilty. McGinniss, like Malcolm after him, was attempting something few nonfiction authors ever do: deciding whether someone is guilty of a heinous crime. McGinniss's book, *Fatal Vision,* became a best-seller in 1983.

Contrary to MacDonald's expectations, however, McGinniss's story, in the form of a lively true-crime narrative, was not a flattering portrait of MacDonald at all. It became an investigation, and the investigation steadily built a case against him. Ultimately, McGinniss suggested that MacDonald had killed his family in a fury of psychotic rage as a result of ingesting amphetamines. In 1984, MacDonald sued McGinniss for breach of contract, including "journalistic distortion." Following a mistrial in 1987 because one juror refused to participate in jury discussions, the breach-of-contract suit was settled out of court for $325,000.

When asked by another reporter if he felt that he betrayed MacDonald, McGinniss replied: "My only obligation from the beginning was to tell the truth."[5] Malcolm reprinted this exchange, although she had little use for McGinniss's brand of truth. But near the end of her book she relates a long anecdote that reflects badly on MacDonald, whom she had come to like. In setting the stage for relating this riveting anecdote, Malcolm almost resentfully observed: "In the course of preparing his book about a murderer who stubbornly refused to exhibit any of the traits one associates with people who kill, and whose past seemed to yield up nothing more ominous than a banal history of promiscuity, McGinniss finally struck gold."[6]

Consistent with her theme of betrayal, Malcolm noted that one of MacDonald's female friends—one of many people whom MacDonald had urged McGinniss to interview—had "betrayed" him by reporting a past incident where she perceived that MacDonald had a violent, cruel streak. Malcolm did not credit the woman for coming forward with her story, however, but instead sneered at her for betraying MacDonald. The friend was an older woman with whom MacDonald had had a love affair. After meeting her, McGinniss wrote this leisurely passage about the time the older woman had spent with MacDonald in the summer of 1971, not long after his family was murdered. Like a lot of young, single men at the time, MacDonald had moved to southern California to start life anew.

McGinniss wrote:

> I learned also that later that summer, not long after MacDonald had taken up residence in Huntington Beach, he received a visit from a close friend of his mother's—a woman he had known since childhood. She brought her 10-year-old son with her.
>
> During the course of the visit, which extended over a period of weeks, Jeffrey MacDonald became sexually intimate with his mother's friend. He himself had told me about this during one of

my visits to Terminal Island. Later, in another part of the country, I located the woman and she confirmed that the story was true, though she was a bit chagrined that he had chosen to make me aware of it.[7]

When McGinniss asked why she had ended the affair with MacDonald, she explained that she had left abruptly because MacDonald had so frightened her son with violent outbursts and threats toward him that she had become scared herself. There were two incidents in particular where MacDonald lost his temper over the boy's perceived misbehavior. McGinniss wrote that, according to the woman, the first incident "occurred when MacDonald—angered by the boy's misbehavior inside his apartment—had carried him outside and dangled him by the feet over the edge of the dock, threatening to drop him head first into the water."[8]

The second incident, the woman told McGinniss, "had occurred later in the summer when she, Jeff, and her son were out for a cruise on her boat. Again, the boy had done something to anger MacDonald. This time, the woman said, MacDonald had grabbed the boy and had told him, in an even more furious and more threatening tone, that upon returning to shore he was going to take the boy's head and hold it over the front of the boat and crush his skull against the dock."[9]

Years later, McGinniss spoke to the boy, who was then attending an Ivy League college. "You have to understand," the boy said, "my parents were divorced and when I was growing up, I hardly ever saw my father. So Jeff was not just like a friend, or even a big brother. Jeff was God to me at that point."[10] In that context, the boy said, the first incident "had not been unduly alarming. Perhaps just a form of roughhousing that had gone a little too far." But the second episode—the scene on the boat—he said, "I remember with real terror to this day." He said that he could not recall what in particular he had done to so anger MacDonald, "but he came at me, yelling, and I remember kind of a fire in his eyes. It *really, really* was scary. I didn't know what he was going to do. In fact, what he did was to throw me in the water—he threw me off the side of the boat while it was moving and I can remember actually feeling relieved that he hadn't done anything more."[11]

Reflecting on that incident, the boy added: "I will never forget that look in his eyes. You know, maybe as a kid you perceive things more directly, in a way, than you do as an adult. But ever since that moment on the boat I believed that he must have been guilty. Just from seeing that kind of fire in his eyes. And I did not want to stay around him anymore. I was very frightened and I told my mother I wanted to go home right away. And we did."[12]

Curiously, in her book, Malcolm omitted one short paragraph from this long passage—the paragraph in which the young man suggests that MacDonald was "God" to him, a factor that made MacDonald's behavior even more inexplicable. What really happened that summer? Malcolm felt the woman had betrayed MacDonald because she talked to McGinniss. But was the woman's story true? Malcolm conceded that "something evidently *had* happened on the boat to upset the boy and to cause his mother, ten years later, to talk about it to a journalist."[13] But what? By letter, she asked this of MacDonald, who deflected the question and directed his anger at McGinniss for having discovered the "one other time"—other than the time he was accused of murdering his family—that his "latent violence was uncovered." In his letter, MacDonald wrote, "McGinniss had to depict me that way to justify his Judas-style of friendship, and so he simply takes normal events and concocts evil in them."[14] That accusation was disingenuous of MacDonald. McGinniss had spent much of his very long book foreshadowing MacDonald's troubled character. And it is doubly disingenuous for Malcolm to quote this episode uncritically, because she, too, presumably had read *Fatal Vision,* and she therefore knew the context of the story of the boat incident. McGinniss had brought the incident up immediately after relating how MacDonald, during the same summer that he had the affair with the older woman, had had sexual relations on a cross-country trip with the sixteen-year-old daughter of friends.

MacDonald, in a letter to Bob Keeler of *Newsday,* which Malcolm quoted in her book, called what McGinniss wrote of this boy-in-the-boat incident "an absolute fabrication," echoing what he had told Mike Wallace of *60 Minutes:* "That never happened. It is a lie."[15] Keeler then called the mother, who confirmed to him that the incident had happened. Malcolm apparently did not reach out to the mother. The matter was brought up in maneuverings before the breach-of-contract trial, but not at trial, and therefore the participants were not subjected to any type of cross-examination to uncover the legal truth of their assertions.

Based on MacDonald's explanation, Malcolm bent over backwards to give MacDonald the benefit of the doubt. The boy-in-the-boat incident, she wrote breezily, was "another illustration of the difficulty of knowing the truth about anything."[16] As if to minimize the recollections of two participants—the boy and his mother—Malcolm jauntily dismissed this anecdote: "One could spend years studying it, as investigators spent years working over the MacDonald murders, and end up with no certain answer to the question of what 'really' happened."[17] By equating the incident on the boat to the murder trial, she diminished the official finding of MacDonald's guilt. Then she misstated the essence of the boating incident, ignoring its gravity by pointing out that MacDonald's actions that day did not amount to all that much: "The question is not who committed the crime, but whether a crime was committed at all," she wrote. Here she misses McGinniss's point. McGinniss's purpose in relating the incident was to show that there was a dark underside to MacDonald's character. But based on these conflicting recollections, Malcolm gave up on the possibility of ever knowing the truth. "Only if MacDonald should confess to the murders," she wrote, "or if someone else should be revealed as the murderer, will we come any closer to being able to judge what happened in the boat."[18]

If two journalists, McGinniss and Malcolm, can each conduct what he or she believes is meticulous research and come to completely different conclusions, what does this say about the truth-seeking apparatus of the journalistic enterprise? How is it possible for journalists to judge facts fairly? In this instance, it seems like it would be hard for Malcolm to reach the conclusions that she did unless she was predisposed to one of the characters and unsympathetic to the other. Malcolm saved her venom for McGinniss, believing he was a false friend and that he had deceived MacDonald for his own selfish purposes. McGinniss, she decided, was the betrayer, because he had lulled MacDonald into thinking he was a sympathetic friend. It did not matter to her that MacDonald had signed a consent agreement. She concluded that McGinniss was the sleazy one, not MacDonald, the man who was convicted of murdering his wife and children.

Malcolm even mocked McGinniss for his ambitions to get the inside story—deriding "the avid interest of some us in being 'insiders' or in getting the 'inside' view of things."[19] When they were still on speaking terms, McGinniss had told Malcolm that he wished to avoid superficiality and did not want to be "in the street interviewing the survivors of fires."[20] But she did not accept that commendable reportorial instinct. "Of course," she wrote,

McGinniss wanted to be "in the burning house itself." So naturally, he jumped at the opportunity when MacDonald offered him the chance to write a book from the perspective of the defense team, with whom he would live and to whose strategies and deliberations he would be privy.

In order to obtain this unprecedented access, McGinniss accepted a condition—a condition, wrote Malcolm, "that another writer might have found unacceptable—namely, that he give MacDonald a share of the book's proceeds."[21] Malcolm did not explore the morality of this arrangement. After all, it *was* MacDonald's life and his story. Why shouldn't McGinniss allow him to profit from his own story? But she did reflect in a surprising way on why subjects talk to writers. The reason, she wrote, is that subjects live in "fear of being found uninteresting."[22] And so for her, the MacDonald-McGinniss pairing represents a "grossly magnified version of the normal journalistic encounter." In her view, McGinniss shifted his attention from MacDonald to the "rhetorically superior story of the prosecution."

Here, she indulged again in one of her overgeneralizations: "The writer ultimately tires of the subject's self-serving story, and substitutes a story of his own. The story of a subject and writer is the Scheherazade story with a bad ending: in almost no case does the subject manage to, as it were, save himself."[23] The allusion to Scheherazade is obscure though enlightening, as it refers to the tale of a king who would marry a new wife every day, have her beheaded, and then marry again. By the time the lovely and cunning Scheherazade volunteers to spend one night with him, he has killed three thousand virgins. The king lies awake as Scheherazade tells him story after story throughout the night until dawn. And so the king keeps Scheherazade alive, eagerly anticipating each new story, until, 1,001 adventurous nights and three sons later, she has entertained and educated the king in morality and kindness, and he makes her his queen. Another story resembling Scheherazade, that of Jeffrey Masson talking on and on to Malcolm, ended badly for him as she tired of him and substituted a story of her own. But Malcolm did not mention this, even though Masson accused her of deceptions not unlike those that McGinniss was accused of perpetrating on MacDonald.

In August 1987, a federal judge in San Francisco dismissed Masson's lawsuit against Malcolm and her publishers on a summary judgment motion. A summary judgment dismissal means the defendant demonstrated to the judge's satisfaction that the plaintiff could not possibly win his case at trial. The judge ruled that there was no basis for the lawsuit because there was no actual malice; in other words, he felt there was no evidence that Malcolm and her codefendants "entertained serious doubts about the truth of the disputed passages."[24] Masson appealed the summary judgment, and four and a half months after *The Journalist and the Murderer* ran in the *New Yorker,* the U.S. Court of Appeals for the Ninth Circuit ruled against him, but the sharp dissent from Judge Alex Kozinski, an unconventional and irrepressible jurist who used this occasion to write what amounted to a treatise on accurate quotations, ensured that the case would live on. Ultimately, the U.S. Supreme Court decided to hear Masson's appeal.

Shortly after the summary judgment had been granted in her case, Malcolm received a form letter from Daniel Kornstein, the New York lawyer who had represented Joe McGinniss. MacDonald's lawsuit against McGinniss had been resolved, and stories about the trial had been in the newspapers in the summer of 1987. Malcolm apparently had missed the stories and said that she learned of the case only after the trial had ended. In his letter, sent to about two dozen journalists, including me, Kornstein wrote: "For the first time, a disgruntled subject has been permitted to sue a writer on grounds that render irrelevant the truth or falsity of what was published." He wished to alert the press to MacDonald's lawsuit, which, he said, suggested that newspaper and magazine reporters, as well as authors, "can and will be sued for writing truthful but unflattering articles."

Her interest piqued, Malcolm got to work, apparently not viewing her absence at the trial as a handicap. She pored over transcripts and interviewed certain participants, but not all of them. Not having attended either MacDonald's murder trial or the trial based on the lawsuit between MacDonald and McGinniss, she produced a secondhand account, and a close reading of her book shows that she selectively chose what evidence to use and what to discard. What interested her in the lawsuit of Jeffrey MacDonald against Joe McGinniss, she wrote, perhaps disingenuously, in an e-mail message years later to a *New York Times* reporter, was "its larger-than-life example of journalistic betrayal," which "offered a way of writing about a chronic, if little discussed, ethical dilemma of journalism."[25]

Though apparently captivated by Jeffrey MacDonald, she never uncovered evidence to exonerate him, neither in *The Journalist and the Murderer* nor in a *New Yorker* profile published much later. In the later piece, which was based on her interview with MacDonald when he was in federal prison, she coyly confessed that she had "once written about him" before.[26] MacDonald "did not say anything remarkable" during the interview, she reported; nonetheless, "the evidence of his guilt grows increasingly elusive." The interview story ended with another cryptic allusion to truth: "Our talk had been friendly and easy; we parted a little reluctantly, as people do who have enjoyed each other's company. 'Look beneath the veneer,' he said—something he had said several times earlier, possibly speaking about himself as well as about the prison, expressing a kind of Platonism that tells us not to trust our senses, that the truth of things is always hidden behind a false front."[27] Malcolm concluded that journalists, like anthropologists, sociologists, and psychoanalysts, "prefer to believe that the front is authentic and the truth of things is written on it—sometimes in a very pale hand, but there to see for those who care to look."[28]

As fond as she appeared to become of MacDonald, Malcolm seemed to like his lawyer, Gary Bostwick, even more. In her second trial with Jeffrey Masson, she hired Bostwick to represent her, and he did so successfully. When she first met him, Bostwick struck her as a man who, though of unexceptional appearance, was of exceptional decency, good humor, and quickness of mind.[29] When she went to interview him, she "knew it wasn't only the fine California climate" that was giving her "such a feeling of well-being." Again, reflecting on her own position as a reporter, she rhapsodized, "The metaphor of the love affair applies to both sides of the journalist-subject equation, and the journalist is no less susceptible than the subject to its pleasures and excitements."[30]

In stark contrast, Kornstein, she thought, was a loser, an impolite nerd and a name dropper. Of course, he was the proximate cause for *The Journalist and the Murderer* in that, without him, Malcolm may never have known about the McGinniss-MacDonald feud, and she never would have written the book. But Kornstein decided not to cooperate with her. For Malcolm, the one incident that revealed Kornstein's character occurred at trial, where, she wrote, he had "frequently humiliated a young associate."[31] One time, the associate made what Kornstein perceived as a mistake while examining a witness, and "Kornstein peremptorily ordered him to sit down." Whatever happened that day in court, Malcolm could not have seen it. She had to rely on the transcript (and transcripts do not convey subjective states of mind; for instance, a transcript would never say a lawyer humiliated a colleague) and the accounts of others who were at the trial. In this case, she relied on what some jurors told her afterward.

In any case, her story of the trial is totally at odds with Kornstein's and McGinniss's recollection of the trial. When the three different versions are juxtaposed, they resemble a *Rashomon*-like story in which each participant recalls a distinctly different account of what happened. Shortly after Malcolm's articles appeared in the *New Yorker,* Kornstein came to his own defense in the inaugural issue of the Cardozo Law School's *Studies in Law and Literature:* "The trial she wrote about bore little resemblance to the trial I was involved in," he wrote.[32] In his methodical, lawyerly fashion, Kornstein presented a case against Malcolm. He claimed that rather than relying on the adversarial process as a means of hammering out the truth, Malcolm presented one side, her side, "without the benefit of an adversarial testing or cross-examination."[33] In fairness to Malcolm, she is a journalist, not a lawyer, and she is not bound by the rules of adversarial proceedings.

Furthermore, Joe McGinniss, in his epilogue to the 1989 revised edition of *Fatal Vision,* turned the tables and defended his lawyer. Reacting to Malcolm's assertion that Kornstein had humiliated his associate, McGinniss wrote, "This is, quite simply, not true."[34] In his own defense, Kornstein elaborated: "The only colleague who tried the case with me is Mark Platt, who is 40 years old (I am 42) and has more gray hair than I do. He occupies the office next to mine in our firm, and we have an excellent working relationship. During the seven weeks we were out in Los Angeles trying the case we worked closely and well together, without the slightest strain despite a steady diet of 18- and 20-hour workdays."[35]

Without a videotape to provide a more nuanced record of the trial, there is just no way to reconcile Malcolm's account of Kornstein's behavior with the accounts of McGinniss and Kornstein. However, we probably should give greater weight to their accounts than to hers, as self-interested as they might seem, simply because they were in court at the time and she was not, and she received her information secondhand.

McGinniss, in the same epilogue to the revised *Fatal Vision,* drew from the ideas of other writers to rebut some of Malcolm's other conclusions. In a reproof to Malcolm, he began with a literary touch, quoting the poet Robert Lowell: "Yet why not tell it like it happened?"[36] McGinniss then questioned Malcolm's basic premise, that journalists invariably practice deception with their subjects, and invoked people whom he believed were authorities to demonstrate that his journalistic methods were effective. He quoted Gay Talese, who wrote in the preface to his 1970 collection of profiles, *Fame and Obscurity:* "I try to follow my subjects unobtrusively while observing them in revealing situations."[37] Then he quoted Tom Wolfe, who in his 1979 introduction to *The New Journalism* wrote: "Most good journalists who hope to get inside someone else's world and stay there awhile come on very softly and do not bombard their subjects with questions. . . . Your main problem as a reporter is, simply, managing to stay with whomever you are writing about long enough for the scene to take place before your own eyes. There are no rules or craft secrets . . . that will help a man pull this off; it is completely a test of his personality."

Comparing the reporter-subject relationship to Heisenberg's uncertainty principle in physics, McGinniss noted that the reporter's very presence inevitably changes the way a subject behaves. "His goal should be to minimize this alteration," McGinniss wrote.[38] Finally, McGinniss summoned up a delightful quote from Marshall Frady, who had written about Billy Graham, George Wallace, and Wilbur Mills: "I like 'em all when I'm with 'em. It's only when I sit down at the typewriter that I realize what sons of bitches they really are."[39]

In defense of his client, Kornstein relied on a transcript for the retelling of an October 1980 meeting between McGinniss, Mac-Donald's criminal lawyer, and the lawyer's assistant. This meeting should have sent loud warning signals, making it clear to MacDonald's team that McGinniss did not necessarily believe in MacDonald's innocence. The contents of the meeting were related at the breach-of-contract trial. At the 1980 meeting, the lawyer's assistant, showing concern about McGinniss's attitude, had asked: "You don't think there is any chance that Jeff is guilty?" McGinniss replied, "I don't know what to think." The assistant then said, "But don't you think you have a moral obligation to Jeff?" McGinniss responded, "I think I have a moral obligation to the truth."[40]

Malcolm drew conclusions from the MacDonald-McGinniss trial record with which other reporters firmly disagreed. She described McGinniss as falling apart on cross-examination, as being "mauled" until there was little left of him, as having had his "liver ravaged."[41] Other reporters, who had actually attended the trial, saw something else. A reporter for the *Long Beach Press Telegram* said that "McGinniss withstood nearly six hours of aggressive questioning." A reporter for *American Lawyer* wrote that McGinniss responded in a "soft, almost academic manner."[42]

Many prominent authors, including J. Anthony Lukas, Victor Navasky, Tom Wolfe, Jimmy Breslin, Joseph Wambaugh, and William Buckley, Jr., either testified for McGinniss or were prepared to do so. In his trial testimony and later in an interview in the *Columbia Journalism Review,* Wambaugh said that MacDonald was someone "who must manipulate his interviewer as he must manipulate everyone in his life."[43] The unstated premise was that MacDonald must have also conned Malcolm.

We will never know. We do know, however, that Malcolm turned on Kornstein, who had been so helpful to her, who provided the initial tip for her book. It was her betrayal, if you will, proof of her point that you must always betray someone in writing an article. We also know that she was unpleasant to Bob Keeler, the reporter from *Newsday* who tried to help her. Keeler had covered the MacDonald case since 1973, and despite his encyclopedic knowledge of it, his book on the murder trial never got published. Keeler keeps popping up in Malcolm's narrative. At one time, she seems to criticize him for asking "blunt" questions.[44] At another point, she relates how, as she was leaving an interview with him, Keeler, "with his irrepressible desire to be helpful,"[45] gave her a large loose-leaf notebook containing the transcripts of his interviews with MacDonald, McGinniss, and others for an article that appeared in *Newsday*'s magazine. "I had not asked for it," Malcolm wrote, "and felt there was something almost illicit about having it in my possession."[46]

His gesture was an "affront" to her pride: "An interview, after all," Malcolm wrote, "is only as good as the journalist who conducts it, and I felt—to put it bluntly—that Keeler, with his prepared questions and his newspaper-reporter's directness, would not get from his subjects the kind of authentic responses that I try to elicit from mine with a more Japanese technique."[47] Then, explaining at least what she meant by her "Japanese technique," she used Keeler as a vehicle to tell a self-deprecating story about herself, suggesting her own limitations:

When I finally read Keeler's transcripts, however, I was in for a surprise and an illumination. MacDonald and McGinniss had said exactly the same things to the unsubtle Keeler that they had said to me. It hadn't made the slightest difference that Keeler had read from a list of prepared questions and I had acted as if I were passing the time of day. From Keeler's blue book I learned the same truth about subjects that the analyst learns about patients: they will tell their story to anyone who will listen to it, and the story will not be affected by the behavior or personality of the listener; just as ("good enough") analysts are interchangeable, so are journalists. My McGinniss and Keeler's McGinniss were the same person, and so were my MacDonald and Keeler's MacDonald and McGinniss's MacDonald. The subject, like the patient, dominates the relationship and calls the shots. The journalist cannot create his subjects any more than the analyst can create his patients.[48]

This is an end-of-book conversion for Malcolm, an about-face that throws into doubt her arresting and famous opening to *The Journalist and the Murderer:* "Every journalist who is not too stupid or too full of himself to notice what is going on knows that what he does is morally indefensible." The journalist, she said, "is a kind of confidence man, preying on people's vanity, ignorance or loneliness, gaining their trust and betraying them without remorse."[49]

In the early pages of *The Silent Woman: Sylvia Plath & Ted Hughes,* which she published in 1994, Malcolm reflected on biography as an art form: "Biography is the medium through which the remaining secrets of the famous dead are taken from them and dumped out in full view of the world. The biographer at work, indeed, is like the professional burglar, breaking into a house, rifling through certain drawers that he has good reason to think contain the jewelry and money, and triumphantly bearing his loot away. The voyeurism and busybodyism that impel writers and readers of biography alike are obscured by an apparatus of scholarship designed to give the enterprise an appearance of bank-like blandness and solidity."[50] The biographer, she continued, is a transgressor, and "there is no length he will not go to, and the more his book reflects his industry the more the reader believes that he is having an elevating literary experience, rather than simply listening to backstairs gossip and reading other people's mail."

In a world where journalists are perceived as conmen and biographers as transgressors, Malcolm placed her trust in the law. In the afterword of *The Journalist and the Murderer,* she wrote enthusiastically of lawsuit therapy: "Of pleasurable reading experience there may be none greater than that afforded by a legal document written on one's behalf. A lawyer will argue for you as you could never argue for yourself, and, with his lawyer's rhetoric, give you a feeling of certitude that you could never obtain for yourself from the language of everyday discourse. People who have never sued anyone or been sued have missed a narcissistic pleasure that is not quite like any other."[51]

She then related how she had experienced "this pleasure" when Jeffrey Masson sued her. She was drawn to the legal documents "as if to a forbidden treat," and she would read the legal papers "like a child reading a favorite story over and over again." Malcolm picked up this same theme at the very start of her latest book, *The Crime of Sheila McGough,* as she ruminated anew on the same truth in her well-crafted but fanciful flights of prose: "The transcripts of trials at law—even of routine criminal prosecutions and tiresome civil disputes—are exciting to read. They record contests of wit and will that have the stylized structure and dire aura of duels before dawn. The reader feels as if he has been brought to the clearing and can smell the wet grass; at the end, as the sky begins to show more light and the doctor is stanching a wound, he takes away a sense of having attended a momentous, if brutal and inconclusive, occasion."[52]

The law's demand "that witnesses speak 'nothing but the truth,'" she continued, "is a demand no witness can fulfill. It runs counter to the law of language, which proscribes unregulated truth-telling and requires that our utterances tell coherent, and thus never merely true, stories." Outside the courtroom, she observed, there is another truth:

> The line between narration and lying is a pretty clear one. As we talk to each other, we constantly make little adjustments to the cut of the truth in order to comply with our listeners' expectation that we will guide them to the point of what we are saying. If we spoke the whole truth, which has no point—which is, in fact, shiningly innocent of a point—we would quickly lose our listeners' attention. The person who insists on speaking the whole truth, who painfully spells out every last detail of an action and interrupts his wife to say it was Tuesday, not Wednesday, and the gunman was wearing a Borsalino, not a fedora, is not honored for his honesty but is shunned for his tiresomeness. In a courtroom however, he would be one of the few people who could withstand cross-examination, who would not be caught in the web of one or another of the small untruths most of us mechanically tell in order that communication be a swift, clear river rather than a sluggish, obstructed stream.[53]

Taken together, Malcolm's oracular pronouncements on truth cancel, overlap, and contradict one another. Her writing, as remarkable as it is, cracks into splinters under close inspection, showing the futility of trying to formulate a grand scheme where journalism and truth fit easily together.

═══════════════◇═══════════════

NINE

LOOKING FORWARD

Before radio, before television, before the Internet, and before pollsters took the national temperature on every subject, Walter Lippmann found that the cacophony of modern life was daunting and often overwhelming. The real environment was "altogether too big, too complex, and too fleeting for direct acquaintance," he wrote in *Public Opinion* in 1922.[1] He called the idea that each of us must acquire a competent opinion about all public affairs an "intolerable and unworkable fiction."[2] Moreover, he believed that the public was not able to govern itself and was not even interested in self-governing, a view which would surely today earn him the label "elitist." For Lippmann, questions of substance were best decided by well-trained experts—whom he called knowledgeable administrators who had access to reliable information.

A new generation of journalists challenged the basic premises of their craft in the 1960s, seeking different ways of reporting their world. To make sense of the turmoil and confusion of that era, Tom Wolfe and others developed narrative methods that shattered the rules. They sought to find interior truths. Although they described what a person did, it was more important to know what the newsmaker *thought*.

Others borrowed the techniques pioneered by the new journalists, and they are still in wide use. A front-page story on the sex trade in San Francisco that appeared in the *San Francisco Chronicle* in 2006, for example, began:

> At 1 A.M., the bell rang. You Mi Kim rushed with eight other
> Korean masseuses to the barren front lobby of Sun Spa in San
> Francisco. The women lined up on an L-shaped couch in their
> lingerie and waited for the customer to choose.
>
> "Don't pick me, don't pick me," You Mi thought, forcing a
> smile.

The reporter was not there to ask You Mi what she felt at the
time or if she "forced" a smile. This was a gripping and evocative
account of how a young Korean, who spoke no English, had been
forced into the sex trade. The story presented an interior truth.
The *Chronicle* went to great length to verify what it could, but it
acknowledged that the story was told by You Mi Kim to the reporter through a Korean interpreter "and is You Mi's version of
events. The shadowy nature of the sex-trafficking industry made
it difficult to locate traffickers and co-workers who were willing
to go on the record to corroborate You Mi's story."[3]

The "new journalism" represented one way of conveying a
kind of truth. So too did another approach, "precision journalism," introduced by Philip Meyer, a reporter turned academic.
Precision journalism is at the opposite end of the spectrum from
"new journalism." Meyer passionately and persuasively urged
journalists to behave more like social scientists: the thesis of his
book, *Precision Journalism,* he wrote, was "that we journalists
would be wrong less often if we adapted to our own use some of
the research tools of the social scientists."[4]

Trend stories relying on two or three anecdotes, he said, were
flawed. He reasoned that journalists are "overly susceptible to an-
ecdotal evidence": "Anecdotes make good reading, and we are
right to use them whenever we can," he wrote. "But we often forget to remind our readers—and ourselves—of the folly of gener-

alizing from a few interesting cases."[5] With the zeal of a converted academic, Meyer pointed out that social scientists were able to digest vast amounts of data, thanks to the availability of computers. Journalists who emulated social scientists would be able to see important stories that were otherwise not apparent. They would be able to find the news, rather than report on what others found, and then report it more accurately, taking greater amounts of data into account. As a result, the use of social science techniques in news reporting has grown substantially over the years. But the techniques of precision journalism still account for only a small fraction of news stories.

Just as in the 1920s, when Lippmann was writing, and the 1960s, both times of tumult and transformation, we are now at a watershed in journalism. Journalism as we know it in fact may not be sufficient in a world so swiftly changing. For instance, today's bloggers are animated by a different (more democratic) spirit than affected Lippmann. The bloggers, "the poster children for a society that has now been nurtured on postmodern rather than Enlightenment sensibilities," as Jane Singer wrote, open up their space for "all comers to post what they know or think."[6]

Melissa Wall, who teaches at the Northridge campus of California State University, described blogging about current events as a "new genre of journalism—offering news that features a narrative style characterized by personalization and an emphasis on non-institutional status; audience participation in context creation; and story forms that are fragmented and interdependent with other websites." The blogging movement is strenuously testing the traditional values of journalism, which respects detachment and neutrality. The voice of the blogger who comments on current events is, Wall wrote, "personalized, opinionated and often one-sided."[7] The primacy of the individual was seized upon by *Time* magazine, which named "you" its highly publicized 2006 person of the year "for seizing the reins of the global media, for founding and framing the new digital democracy, for working for nothing and beating the pros at their own game."[8]

Bloggers clearly differ from traditional journalists in their notion of how to attain truth. "Bloggers see themselves as the opposite of gatekeepers," wrote Jane Singer.[9] "They do not see truth as resting on the decision of one autonomous individual or group of individuals within a news organization or anywhere else. Instead, bloggers see truth as emerging from shared, collective knowledge—from an electronically enabled marketplace of ideas." Taking its cues from social networking sites and the Internet phenomenon YouTube, blogging depends heavily on the audience's urge to participate, an urge that mainstream journalism was late in understanding.

Early on, at least one reporter did recognize the importance of having an audience that was active instead of passive. In a speech he gave honoring the 1979 winners of the Pulitzer Prize at the National Press Club in Washington, D.C., David Broder, the epitome of establishment reporters and the outstanding political writer for the *Washington Post,* began by criticizing the slogan of the *New York Times,* where Broder had worked earlier in his career. Although he praised "All the News That's Fit to Print" as a "great" slogan, he contended that it also was a "fraud." Neither the *Times* nor the *Post*—or any other newspaper or network news show— he said, "has space or time to deal with all the actions taken and all the words uttered in the city of Washington with significance for some of its readers or viewers." "And that says nothing of what is happening every day in the rest of the country and the world."[10]

Broder was remarkably shrewd in questioning the gatekeeping role of the press, especially considering that he was speaking to a pre-Internet audience. He said: "If we treated our audience with the respect its members deserve, and gave them an accurate understanding of the pressures of time and space under which we work, we could acknowledge the inherent limitations and imperfections of our work—instead of reacting defensively when they are pointed out." He favored full disclosure, letting the audience in on how journalistic decisions are made:

> We could say plainly what we all know to be the case, that the process of selecting what the reader reads involves not just objective facts but subjective judgments, personal values, and yes, prejudices. Instead of promising "All the News That's Fit to Print," I would like to see us say—over and over, until the point has been made—that the newspaper that drops on your doorstep is a partial, hasty, incomplete, inevitably somewhat flawed and inaccurate rendering of some of the things we have heard about in the past 24 hours—distorted, despite our best efforts to eliminate gross bias, by the very process of compression that makes it possible for you to lift it from the doorstep and read it in about an hour. If we labeled the product accurately, then we could immediately add: "But it's the best we could do under the circumstances, and we will be back tomorrow with a corrected and updated version."[11]

Broder was prescient in welcoming audience input: "If we did that, I suspect, not only would we feel less inhibited about correcting and updating our own stories, we might even encourage the readers to contribute their own information and understanding to the process. We might even find ourselves acknowledging something most of us find hard to accept: that they have something to tell us, as well as to hear from us. And if those readers felt that they were part of a communications process in which they were participants and not just passive consumers, then they might more easily understand that their freedoms—and not just ours—

are endangered when the search warrants and subpoenas are visited on the press."[12]

Too often, journalists do not let readers in on their secrets. "If journalists are to be truth seekers," wrote Bill Kovach and Tom Rosenstiel in *The Elements of Journalism,* "it must follow that they be honest and truthful with their audiences, too—that they be truth presenters. If nothing else, this responsibility requires that journalists be as open and honest with audiences as they can about what they know and what they don't."[13] Years earlier, in his introduction to the collection of essays entitled *Between Fact and Fiction: The Problem of Journalism,* Ed Epstein described the journalist's dilemma, stating that though journalists can faithfully be the conveyors of a message to an audience, the message might be false. Alternatively, they can recast the message into what they think is true, but this might lead to distortion. "In neither case," Epstein observed, "can journalists be certain of either the truth or the intended purpose of what they publish."[14] To some degree, he continued, "the tension of the dilemma could be alleviated if journalists gave up the pretense of being establishers of truth, recognized themselves as agents for others who desired to disclose information, and clearly labeled the circumstances and interests behind the information they reported so that it could be intelligently evaluated."[15]

As Broder pointed out, the audience sometimes gets forgotten in the author-audience equation. Implicit in his vision is that readers and viewers—not just journalists—need to be better at what they do. My friend Evan Cornog, picking up this theme in an essay entitled "Let's Blame the Readers," published in the *Columbia Journalism Review,* posed questions that are too infrequently addressed: "Why are so many people avoiding the hard task of keeping themselves informed about what is going on in their government and society? Why is ignorance so widespread at a time when higher education is more widely pursued than ever before?" After exploring some root causes of the discouraging state of public awareness, Cornog proposed that journalism, with its power to examine any aspect of society, "can in this way set in motion a debate that may help it put its own house in better order."[16]

But journalism is still, as Thomas Griffith characterized it half a century ago in *The Waist-High Culture,* "history on the run." Journalists need to be much more aware of their relative strengths and shortcomings, and they need to let the readers and viewers in on their secrets. After all, as Griffith remarked : "If journalism is sometimes inaccurate and often inadequate, ignorance would not be preferable."[17]

NOTES

CHAPTER ONE

1. See Tom Goldstein, "Lies, Damn Lies and Jayson Blair's Lies," San Francisco Chronicle, May 25, 2003, Insight, 1.

2. James Boswell, *The Life of Samuel Johnson* (New York: Random House, 1952), 44.

3. H. L. Mencken, "A Neglected Anniversary," *New York Evening Mail,* December 28, 1917, 9.

4. Allan Nevins, *The Gateway to History* (Chicago: Quadrangle Books, 1963), 138.

5. Robin Winks, ed., *The Historian as Detective: Essays on Evidence* (New York: Harper and Row, 1970), 193.

6. Walter Lippmann and Charles Merz, "A Test of the News," *New Republic,* August 4, 1920, 1–43.

7. Christopher Lasch, *The Revolt of the Elites and the Betrayal of Democracy* (New York: W. W. Norton, 1995), 168.

8. Alastair Reid, "Letter from Barcelona," *New Yorker,* December 2, 1961, 137.

9. A. J. Liebling, *The Press,* 2d ed. (New York: Pantheon Books, 1975), 22.

10. John Hersey, "The Legend on the License," *Yale Review* (Autumn 1980), 2.

11. Ibid., 2.

12. "Who Said That?" A Report to the National News Council on the Use of Unidentified Sources, 1983, 2.

13. Janet Cooke, "Jimmy's World," *Washington Post,* September 28, 1980, 1.

14. Ben Bradlee, *A Good Life* (New York: Touchstone, 1995), 445.

15. Ibid., 445.

16. Katharine Graham, *Personal History* (New York: Alfred A. Knopf, 1997), 599.

17. *Royal Commission on the Press, 1947–1949* (London: His Majesty's Stationery Office, 1949), 127.

18. T. S. Matthews, *The Sugar Pill* (New York: Simon and Schuster, 1959), 164.

19. Penn Kimball, "Journalism: Art, Craft, or Profession?" in K. S. Lynn, ed., *The Professions in America* (Boston: Beacon, 1963), 253.

20. *Royal Commission on the Press,* 127.

21. National News Council, *After "Jimmy's World": Tightening Up in Editing* (New York: National News Council, 1981), 55.

22. Ibid., 55.

23. *Crossfire,* CNN, August 1, 1996.

24. Don Van Natta Jr., Adam Liptak, and Clifford J. Levy, "The Miller Case: A Notebook, A Cause, a Jail Cell and a Deal," *New York Times,* October 16, 2005, 1.

25. Edward Wyatt, "Live on 'Oprah': A Memoirist Is Kicked Out of the Book Club," *New York Times,* January 27, 2006, 1.

26. Richard Zoglin, "Some Like It Hot, *Time,* August 9, 1993.

27. *Davis v. Costa-Gavras et al.,* 654 F. Supp. 653 (S.D.N.Y.), 658.

28. Panel discussion, "Docudramas and the Law: 'Truth' and Consequences," Association of the Bar of the City of New York, June 11, 1985.

29. Richard Siklos, "I Cannot Tell a Lie (From an Amplification)," *New York Times,* February 5, 2006, Section 3, 3.

30. Jane Singer, "Truth and Transparency: Bloggers' Challenge to Professional Autonomy in Defining and Enacting Two Journalistic Norms" (Paper presented at the annual meeting, Association for Education in Journalism and Mass Communication, August 2006), 24.

31. Ibid.

32. Chris Mooney, "Blinded by Science: How 'Balanced' Coverage Lets the Fringe Hijack Reality," *Columbia Journalism Review,* November/December 2004, 26.

33. Jonathan Cole, "Academic Freedom under Fire," *Daedalus,* Spring 2005, 11.

34. Deni Elliott, "Journalistic Truth: An Essay Review," *Journal of Mass Media Ethics* 9, no. 3 (1994), 184.

35. Ibid.

36. Kevin Kerrane and Ben Yagoda, eds., *The Art of the Fact* (New York: Scribner, 1997), 14.

37. John Soloski, "News Reporting and Professionalism: Some Constraints on the Reporting of the News," *Media, Culture and Society* 11 (1989), 214.

38. James Stewart, "Consider the Sources," *New York Times Book Review,* July 4, 1999.

39. Ibid.

40. Elizabeth Loftus and Katherine Ketcham, *Witness for the Defense* (New York: St. Martin's Press, 1991), 9.

41. Jack Fuller, *News Values* (Chicago: University of Chicago Press, 1996), 3.

42. Bill Kovach and Tom Rosenstiel, *The Elements of Journalism* (New York: Crown, 2001), 72–73.

43. Edward J. Epstein, *Between Fact and Fiction: The Problem of Journalism* (New York: Vintage Books, 1975), 4.

44. H. L. Mencken, "Newspaper Morals," *Atlantic Monthly,* March 1914, 291.

45. Singer, 14.

46. Ibid.

47. Nancy Gibbs, "Who Owns the Truth?" *Time,* September 27, 2004, 34.

48. *Nightline,* ABC, September 3, 2004.

CHAPTER TWO

1. Thomas F. Burke, Lawyers, Lawsuits and Legal Rights: The Battle over Litigation in American Society (Berkeley: University of California Press, 2002), 2, 24; William Haltom and Michael McCann, Distorting the Law (Chicago: The University of Chicago Press, 2004), 155, 185–187.

2. Burke, *Lawyers, Lawsuits and Legal Rights,* 26.

3. Haltom and McCann, *Distorting the Law,* 208.

4. Ibid., 215.

5. Katharine Seelye, "Agendas Clash in Bid to Alter Law on Product Liability," *New York Times,* September 24, 2006.

6. Burke, *Lawyers, Lawsuits and Legal Rights,* 24; John Nockleby and Shannon Curreri, "100 Years of Conflict: The Past and Future of Tort Retrenchment," *Loyola of Los Angeles Law Review* 38 (2004–2005), 1032.

7. Seelye, "Agendas Clash."

8. Haltom and McCann, *Distorting the Law,* 163.

9. Ibid., 166.

10. Ibid., 165.

11. Ibid., 150.

12. Michael Schudson, "Runaway Juries . . . and Other Made-for-Media Myths," *Columbia Journalism Review,* July/August 2005, 69.

13. Nockleby and Curreri, "100 Years of Conflict," 1090.

14. Nancy Marder, "The Medical Malpractice Debate: The Jury as Scapegoat," *Loyola of Los Angeles Law Review* 38 (2004–2005), 1269.

15. Ibid., 1274.

16. Ibid., 1284.

17. Bob Steele, *RTNDA Communicator,* April 1997, 56.

18. Ibid.

19. Richard A. Epstein, "Privacy, Publication, and the First Amendment: The Dangers of First Amendment Exceptionalism," *Stanford Law Review* 52 (2000), 1029.

20. Ibid., 1031–1032.

21. Robert Maynard Hutchins, *A Free and Responsible Press,* Midway Reprint Series, Robert D. Leigh, ed. (1947; Chicago: University of Chicago Press, 1974), 55.

22. Thomas Griffith, *The Waist-High Culture* (New York: Harper and Brothers, 1959), 69.

23. Max Frankel, "Word and Image: What's New," *New York Times Magazine,* June 18, 1995, 20.

24. *Today Show,* NBC, September 29, 2006.

25. Linda Lightfoot, "Editors Hear the Roar of the Food Lion Case," *American Editor,* January-February 1997.

26. Robin Winks, ed. *The Historian as Detective: Essays on Evidence* (New York: Harper and Row, 1970), xv.

27. Philip Meyer, *Precision Journalism* (Bloomington: Indiana University Press, 1973).

28. Edward J. Epstein, *Between Fact and Fiction: The Problem of Journalism*, x.

29. Ibid., 3.

30. Walter Lippmann, *Public Opinion* (New York: Free Press, 1997), 226.

31. Ibid., 229.

32. "Q & A: Gay Talese," *SI.com*, May 25, 2006.

33. Walter Lippmann, *Liberty and the News* (New York: Harcourt, Brace and Howe, 1920), 79.

34. Ibid., 60; Bill Kovach and Tom Rosenstiel, *The Elements of Journalism* (New York: Crown, 2001), 73; Paul Starr, *The Creation of the Media* (New York: Basic Books, 2004), 396.

35. Lippmann, *Public Opinion,* 227.

36. Jane Singer, "Truth and Transparency: Bloggers' Challenge to Professional Autonomy in Defining and Enacting Two Journalistic Norms," 14; Bill Kovach and Tom Rosenstiel, *The Elements of Journalism* (New York: Crown, 2001), 73.

37. Charles A. Beard, "Written History as an Act of Faith," *American Historical Review* 39, no. 2 (January 1934), 220.

38. Ibid., 226.

39. Singer, *Truth and Transparency,* 14.

40. Naomi Oreskes, "The Scientific Consensus on Climate Change: How Do We Know We're Not Wrong?" in Joseph DiMento and Pamela Doughman, eds., *Climate Change: What It Means for Us, Our Children and Our Grandchildren* (Cambridge: MIT Press, 2007), 18.

41. Ibid., 29.

42. Winks, *The Historian as Detective,* 39.

43. William Roger Lewis, "Introduction," in Robin Winks, ed. *The Oxford History of the British Empire,* vol. 5. (Oxford: Oxford University Press, 1999), xxv.

44. Mark T. Gilderhus, *History and Historians,* 5th ed. (Upper Saddle River, N.J.: Prentice Hall, 2003), 107.

45. Arthur Schlesinger, Jr., "Folly's Antidote," *New York Times,* January 1, 2007, A23.

46. Gilderhus, *History and Historians,* 128.

47. R. G. Collingwood, *The Idea of History,* rev. ed. (Oxford: Oxford University Press, 1994), 249.

48. Winks, *The Historian as Detective,* xiv.

49. Collingwood, *The Idea of History,* 258.

50. Ibid., 259.

51. Winks, *The Historian as Detective,* 39.

52. Louis Menand, "Everybody's an Expert," *New Yorker,* December 5, 2005, 98.

53. Christopher Cerf and Victor Navasky, *The Experts Speak: The Definitive Compendium of Authoritative Misinformation,* 2d ed. (New York: Villard, 1998), xxv.

54. Don Van Natta Jr., Adam Liptak, and Clifford J. Levy, "The Miller Case: A Notebook, a Cause, a Jail Cell and a Deal," *New York Times,* October 16, 2005, 1.

55. Philip Tetlock, *Expert Political Judgment* (Princeton, N.J.: Princeton University Press, 2005), 235.

56. Federal Rules of Evidence, Number 702.

CHAPTER THREE

1. Rosemary Pattenden, "Conceptual versus Pragmatic Approaches to Hearsay," *Modern Law Review* 56, no. 2 (March 1993), 151; John Strong, ed., *McCormick on Evidence,* 5th ed. (St. Paul, Minn.: West, 1999), 372 ff.

2. *Crawford v. Washington,* 541 U.S. 43–44 (2004); Robert Chambers, *The Book of Days* (1969), http://www.thebookofdays.com.

3. *Crawford,* 43–44.

4. Ibid., 59.

5. Strong, *McCormick on Evidence,* 372.

6. Stephen Gillers, "On Knowing the Basic Rules of Advocacy," *New York Times,* February 8, 2004, "Week in Review," 2.

7. Michael Asimow, "Popular Culture and the American Adversarial Ideology" (Paper prepared for symposium, "How Popular Culture Teaches Americans about the Civil Justice System," Loyola School of Law, September 29, 2006), 4.

8. Ibid., 5.

9. Ibid., 19.

10. Robert Bendiner, "The Law and Potter Stewart: An Interview with Justice Potter Stewart," *American Heritage,* December 1983.

11. *People v. Defore,* 150 N.E. 585, 587 (N.Y. 1926).

12. *Miranda v. Arizona,* 384 U.S. 436 (1966).

13. Jack Weinstein, Order and Judgment, *United States v. Louis Eppolito and Stephen Caracappa,* June 30, 2006, 6.

14. Ibid., 74.

15. Geoffrey Stone, "Above the Law: Research Methods, Ethics, and the Law of Privilege," *Sociological Methodology* 32 (2002), 19.

16. Strong, *McCormick on Evidence,* 375; Mark Stevens, *Justice 405 Syllabus,* North Carolina Wesleyan College.

17. Walter Lippmann, *Public Opinion* (New York: Free Press, 1997), 219.

18. Ibid.

19. Leon Sigal, "Sources Make the News," in Robert Karl Manoff and Michael Schudson, eds., *Reading the News* (New York: Pantheon, 1987), 15–16.

20. Michael Gordon and Judith Miller, "Threats and Responses: The Iraqis; U.S. Says Hussein Intensifies Quest for A-Bomb Parts," *New York Times,* September 8, 2002, 1.

21. Ibid.

22. "Letter to the Editor: Judith Miller's Farewell," *New York Times,* November 10, 2005, 28.

23. Michael Massing, "Now They Tell Us," *New York Review of Books,* February 26, 2004, 43.

24. Don Van Natta, Jr., Adam Liptak, and Clifford J. Levy, "The Miller Case: A Notebook, a Cause, a Jail Cell and a Deal," *New York Times,* October 16, 2005, 1.

25. Testimony of Judith Miller, Senate Judiciary Committee, U.S. Senate, October 19, 2005.

26. National Public Radio, *The Connection,* February 3, 2004.

27. Editors' Note, *New York Times,* May 26, 2004, 10.

28. Howell Raines on "The Times and Iraq," note, http://www.poynter.org/forum, May 26, 2004.

29. Jonathan Donnellan and Justin Peacock, "Truth and Consequences: First Amendment Protection for Accurate Reporting on Government Investigations," *New York Law School Law Review* 50 (2005–2006), 240.

30. Ibid., 244.

CHAPTER FOUR

1. Jack Devlin, "Pesticide Spokesmen Accused of 'Lying' on Higher Bird Count," *New York Times,* August 14, 1972, 33.

2. Robert Arbib, Jr., "Foreword: Christmas Bird Count," *American Birds* 26, no. 2 (April 1972), 135–136.

3. *Edwards v. National Audubon Society,* 556 F.2nd 113 (2nd Cir.).

4. Ibid., 120.

5. Ted Glasser, "Objectivity Precludes Responsibility," *Quill,* February 1984, 15.

6. *Edwards,* 120.

7. Ibid.

8. Glasser, "Objectivity Precludes Responsibility," 15.

9. *SPJ FOI Alert* 1, Issue 7, July 19, 1996.

10. *Khawar v. Globe International Inc.,* 79 Cal. Rptr. 2nd 178 (Cal. 1998).

11. Glasser, "Objectivity Precludes Responsibility," 14.

12. John Harris, *Washington Post* online conversation of February 2, 2006.

13. Jeffrey Dworkin, *NPR Ombudsman: "Truth with Edge?"* June 13, 2006.

14. Al Gore, *An Inconvenient Truth* (Emmaus, Pa.: Rodale, 2006), 262–263.

15. Naomi Oreskes, "The Scientific Consensus on Climate Change," *Science* 306 (December 3, 2004), 1686.

16. Naomi Oreskes, "The Scientific Consensus on Climate Change: How Do We Know We're Not Wrong?" in Joseph DiMento and Pamela Doughman, eds., *Climate Change: What It Means for Us, Our Children and Our Grandchildren* (Cambridge: MIT Press, 2007).

17. Maxwell Boykoff and Jules Boykoff, "Balance as Bias: Global Warming and the US Prestige Press," *Global Environmental Change* 14 (2004).

18. Oreskes, "The Scientific Consensus on Climate Change," 6.

19. Ibid., 11.

20. Ibid., 12.

21. Boykoff and Boykoff, "Balance as Bias," 126.

22. Ibid.

23. Gore, *An Inconvenient Truth,* 265.

24. Stephen Schneider's webpage, http://stephenschneider.stanford .edu.

CHAPTER FIVE

1. *Hamlet,* Act III, Scene 2, in *The Riverside Shakespeare,* 2d ed. (New York: Houghton Mifflin, 1997), 1214. See Elizabeth Loftus and Katherine Ketcham, *Witness for the Defense* (New York: St. Martin's Press, 1991), introductory page.

2. Fernand Van Langenhove, *The Growth of a Legend* (New York: G. P. Putnam's, 1916), 1.

3. Ibid., 118.

4. Ibid., 119.

5. Ibid., 119–121.

6. Ibid., 123.

7. Walter Lippmann, *Public Opinion,* 55–56.

8. Edna Buchanan, *New York Times,* May 25, 1991.

9. Gary Wells and Elizabeth Olson, "Eyewitness Testimony," *Annual Review of Psychology* 54 (2003), 277–278.

10. Ibid., 278.

11. Seth Mydans, "Coup May Allow Thais to Take New Tack on Insurgency," *New York Times,* September 24, 2006.

12. Mitchell Stephens, "We're All Postmodern Now," *Columbia Journalism Review,* July/August 2005, 60.

13. Ibid., 61.

14. Ibid., 63.

15. Mark Danner, "Iraq: The Real Election," *New York Review of Books,* April 28, 2005, 41.

16. Ibid.

17. Farnaz Fassihi, "WSJ Reporter Fassihi's E-mail to Friends," *Poynteronline,* September 29, 2004.

18. Phillip Knightley, *The First Casualty: The War Correspondent as Hero and Myth-Maker from the Crimea to Iraq,* 3d ed. (Baltimore: Johns Hopkins University Press, 2004), xi.

19. *Idler,* no. 30 (November 11, 1758).

20. Knightley, *The First Casualty,* xiii.

21. Ian Fisher, "Reporting and Surviving: Iraq's Dangers," *New York Times,* July 18, 2004, "Week in Review," 1.

22. Ian Fisher, "Attack in Iraq: Many Versions Obscure Truth," *New York Times,* April 26, 2004, 1.

23. Matt Singer, "Tales from the Hood: Boredom Abounds in Fairy-Tale Pastiche," *Village Voice,* January 10, 2006.

CHAPTER SIX

1. Plaintiff's complaint, *Carolyn Condit v.* National Enquirer, U.S. District Court, Eastern District of California–Fresno Division, February 21, 2002, 3.

2. *National Enquirer,* August 7, 2001, 1.

3. Tom Goldstein, "Going Respectable," *New York Newsday,* June 24, 1987, Part II, 3.

4. S. Elizabeth Bird, *For Enquiring Minds: A Cultural Study of Supermarket Tabloids* (Knoxville: University of Tennessee Press, 1992), 7.

5. Ibid., 24.

6. "20th Century Great American Business Leaders," www.hbs.edu/leadership/database/leaders/714/.

7. *National Enquirer,* March 2, 1976.

8. Rodney Smolla, *Suing the Press* (Oxford: Oxford University Press, 1986), 100–101.

9. Iain Calder, *The Untold Story: My 20 Years Running the National Enquirer* (New York: Hyperion, 2004), 166.

10. *National Enquirer,* April 6, 1976.

11. Smolla, *Suing the Press,* 104.

12. Laurence Leamer, *King of the Night: The Life of Johnny Carson* (New York: William Morrow, 1989), 325.

13. Ibid.

14. Calder, *The Untold Story,* 169.

15. Ibid., 170.

16. Ibid., 172.

17. "Williams & Connolly: Our Attorneys," www.wc.com.

18. Jim Amidon, "30 Minutes with David Kendall," *Wabash Magazine,* Fall/Winter 2001.

19. Jack Shafer, "I Believe the *National Enquirer,* Why Don't You?" *Slate,* June 11, 2004, www.slate.com/id/2102303.

20. Calder, *The Untold Story,* 212.

21. Suzanne Garment, *Scandal: The Culture of Mistrust in American Politics* (New York: New York Times Books, 1991), 182.

22. Paul Taylor, *See How They Run: Electing the President in an Age of Mediacracy* (New York: Alfred A. Knopf, 1990), 78.

23. Jim McGee and Tom Fiedler, "Miami Woman Is Linked to Hart," *Miami Herald,* May 3, 1987, 1.

24. E. J. Dionne, "Gary Hart: The Elusive Front-Runner," *New York Times Magazine,* May 3, 1987.

25. James Bennet, "Who's Mr. Clean? Washington Nervously Awaits New Deliveries of Dirty Laundry," *New York Times,* September 6, 1998, "Week in Review," 5.

26. Debra Gersh, "Good Journalism or Snooping," *Editor and Publisher,* May 16, 1987, 9.

27. Ibid.

28. Tom Goldstein, "The Press and the Political Candidate," *Miami Herald,* May 10, 1987, C1.

29. Tom Goldstein, "Going Respectable," *New York Newsday,* June 24, 1987, Part II, 3.

30. Andrea Sachs, "Mud and the Mainstream," *Columbia Journalism Review,* May/June 1995, 33.

31. David Broder, "The Summer of My Discontent," *Washington Post,* August 28, 1994, C4.

32. David Lamb, "Into the Realm of Tabloids; Never Before Has Tabloid Journalism Been Such a Growth Industry," *Los Angeles Times,* February 13, 1992, 1.

33. *Nightline,* ABC, October 11, 1995.

34. Calder, *The Untold Story,* 276.

35. Roger Cossack, interview for *Nightline,* ABC, June 30, 2004.

36. *Nightline,* ABC, July 1, 2004.

37. Ibid.

38. Gilbert Cranberg, "Paying for 'News' Taints Justice System," *USA Today,* 14A.

39. David Margolick, "Deputy Tells of Emotions of Simpson," *New York Times,* December 15, 1994, A28.

40. David Margolick, "Simpson Judge Sets Date for Pretrial Hearing

on DNA and Rules on Jail Outburst," *New York Times,* December 20, 1994, A18.

41. Howard Kurtz, "Truth or Tabloid Trash? *New York Times* Quotes *Enquirer* on O.J. Story," *Washington Post,* December 21, 1994, C1.

42. William Glaberson, "*Times* Criticized for Use of Tabloid Account," *New York Times,* December 23, 1994, A11.

43. Advertisement, "The National Enquirer in on a Roll," *New York Times,* April 21, 1997, C20.

44. Donald Trelford, Speech (on file), March 29, 1983.

45. John Tierney, *New York Times Magazine,* April 18, 1993, 64.

46. Michael Wines, "To Fill Notebooks, and Then a Few Bellies," *New York Times,* August 27, 2006, "Week in Review," 1.

CHAPTER SEVEN

1. Douglas Martin, "James W. Carey, Teacher of Journalists, Dies at 71," *New York Times,* May 26, 2006, C11.

2. Jay Mathews, "Just Checking," *New Republic,* May 18, 1992, 16.

3. James Boylan, *Pulitzer's School: Columbia University's School of Journalism, 1903–2003* (New York: Columbia University Press, 2003), 224.

4. "In Remembrance of Jim Carey," http://www.poynter.org/media/mediacast/pub/1019/podcast.asp?id=1019.

5. *Time, Inc. v. Hill,* 385 U.S. 374 (1967), 389.

6. James Rutenberg and Edmund L. Andrews, "Evans Seen Atop List to Head Treasury," *New York Times,* May 27, 2006, 1.

7. Boylan, *Pulitzer's School,* 226.

8. Christopher Scanlan, *Reporting and Writing: Basics for the 21st Century* (Orlando, Fla.: Harcourt College Publishers, 2000), 48.

9. Richard Blow and Ari Posner, "Adventures in Fact Checking: Are You Completely Bald?" *New Republic,* September 26, 1988, 23.

10. S. Elizabeth Bird, *For Enquiring Minds: A Cultural Study of Supermarket Tabloids* (Knoxville: University of Tennessee Press, 1992), 94.

11. Susan Shapiro, "This Paper Has Not Been Fact Checked! A Study of Fact-Checking in American Magazines," Gannett Center for Media Studies, 1989, 6–7.

12. Daniel Okrent, "What Do You Know, and How Do You Know It?" *New York Times,* February 29, 2004.

13. Ibid.

14. Otto Friedrich, "There Are oo Trees in Russia: The Function of Facts in Newsmagazines," *Harper's Magazine,* October 1964, 60.

15. Ibid., 62.

16. Ibid., 63.

17. Ibid.

18. Judith Sheppard, "Playing Defense," *American Journalism Review,* September 1998.

19. *New Yorker,* "Check the Facts: Fact-Checking at *The New Yorker,*" 1988.

20. Joseph Mitchell, *Old Mr. Flood* (San Francisco: MacAdam Cage, 2005), 3; see also Kent MacDougall, Letter to the editor, *Wall Street Journal,* July 2, 1984.

21. Mitchell, *Old Mr. Flood,* xi.

22. Alastair Reid, "Letter from Barcelona," *New Yorker,* December 2, 1961, 137.

23. Joanne Lipman, "At the New Yorker, Editor and a Writer Differ on the 'Facts,'" *Wall Street Journal,* June 18, 1984, 1.

24. Maureen Dowd, "A Writer for the New Yorker Says He Created Composites in Reports," *New York Times,* June 19, 1984, 1.

25. Tom Goldstein, "Gore Flap the Latest in a Series of Clashes between Academic and Press Freedom," *American Editor,* April 2001.

26. Edwin McDowell, "New Yorker Editor Calls Reporting Style Wrong," *New York Times,* July 3, 1984, C9.

27. Mimi Sheraton, *Eating My Words: An Appetite for Life* (New York: Harper Perennial, 2004), 130.

28. "Devouring a Small Country Inn," *Time,* March 12, 1979.

29. Ralph Blumenthal, "Freud Archives Research Chief Removed in Dispute over Yale Talk," *New York Times,* November 9, 1981.

30. Ibid.

31. Slade Metcalf, "He Said, She Said: 'Get It on Tape or Go to Trial' Is the Message from a Recent Supreme Court Decision on Reformatting Quotes," *Folio,* September 1, 1991.

32. *Masson v. New Yorker,* 895 F.2d 1535, 1570 (9th Cir. 1989).

33. David Margolick, "Psychoanalyst Loses Libel Suit Against a New Yorker Reporter," *New York Times,* November 2, 1994, 1.

34. Steve Weinberg, "Why Books Err So Often," *Columbia Journalism Review,* July/August 1998, 52.

35. David Kirkpatrick, "Why Books Are the Hot Medium," *New York Times,* April 25, 2004, Section 4, 1.

36. Edwin McDowell, "Issue and Debate: The Standards of Evidence in Book Publishing," *New York Times,* June 19, 1984, C14.

37. Daniel Okrent, "The Privileges of Opinion, the Obligations of Fact," *New York Times,* March 28, 2004.

38. Adam Cohen, "Can Oprah Change the Phony-Memoir Culture?" *New York Times,* February 14, 2006.

39. Philip K. Howard, *The Death of Common Sense* (New York: Random House, 1995), 130.

40. Richard Lacayo, "Anecdotes Not Antidotes: Philip K. Howard Is Everyone's Favorite Anti-Regulatory Guru, But His Best-Selling Book Is Flawed," *Time,* April 10, 1995.

41. Cohen, "Can Oprah Change the Phony-Memoir Culture?"

42. Weekly Notes, *Bloomberg,* August 27, 2006.

43. Statement on www.FactCheck.org.

CHAPTER EIGHT

1. Janet Malcolm, *The Crime of Sheila McGough* (New York: Vintage Books, 1999), 26.

2. Richard Posner, "In the Fraud Archives," *New Republic,* April 19, 1999, 34.

3. Dinitia Smith, "Another Top 100 List: Now It's Nonfiction," *New York Times,* April 30, 1999, E45.

4. Craig Seligman, "Janet Malcolm: In Her Relentless Pursuit of the Truth She's Left a Few Bodies in Her Wake, but Isn't That Part of a Journalist's Job?" *Salon.com,* February 29, 2000.

5. Janet Malcolm, *The Journalist and the Murderer* (New York: Alfred A. Knopf, 1990), 25.

6. Ibid., 130.

7. Joe McGinniss, *Fatal Vision* (New York: New American Library, 1989), 617.

8. Ibid.

9. Ibid.

10. Ibid., 618.

11. Ibid.

12. Ibid.

13. Malcolm, *The Journalist and the Murderer,* 132.

14. Ibid.

15. Ibid., 133.

16. Ibid., 134.

17. Ibid.

18. Ibid.

19. Ibid., 17.

20. Ibid., 18.

21. Ibid.

22. Ibid., 20.

23. Ibid., 21.

24. *Masson v. New Yorker,* 895 F.2d 1535, 1550 (9th Cir. 1989).

25. David Carr, "A Writer Is Back in the Saddle after His Fall from Grace," *New York Times,* July 28, 2004.

26. Janet Malcolm, "Easy Time: A Glimpse at the Life of Jeffrey Mac-Donald, Who Is Serving Time in a Model Federal Prison," *New Yorker,* October 16, 1995, 99.

27. Ibid., 107.

28. Ibid.

29. Malcolm, *The Journalist and the Murderer,* 42.

30. Ibid., 59.

31. Ibid., 42.

32. Daniel Kornstein, "Twisted Vision: Janet Malcolm's Upside Down View of the *Fatal Vision* Case," *Cardozo Studies in Law and Literature* 1, no. 2 (Autumn 1989), 153.

33. Ibid., 152.

34. McGinniss, *Fatal Vision,* 677.

35. Kornstein, "Twisted Vision," 138–139.

36. McGinniss, *Fatal Vision,* 664.

37. Ibid.

38. Ibid., 665.

39. Ibid.

40. Kornstein, "Twisted Vision," 136.

41. Malcolm, *The Journalist and the Murderer,* 9, 14.

42. Kornstein, "Twisted Vision," 138.

43. Martin Gottlieb, "Dangerous Liaisons: Journalists and Their Sources," *Columbia Journalism Review,* July/August 1989, 25.

44. Malcolm, *The Journalist and the Murderer,* 24.

45. Ibid., 77.

46. Ibid., 98.

47. Ibid.

48. Ibid.

49. Ibid., 3.

50. Janet Malcolm, *The Silent Woman* (New York: Alfred A. Knopf, 1994), 8–9.

51. Malcolm, *The Journalist and the Murderer,* 148.

52. Malcolm, *The Crime of Sheila McGough,* 3.

53. Ibid, 3–4.

CHAPTER NINE

1. Lippmann, *Public Opinion* (New York: Free Press, 1997), 11.

2. Ibid., 18.

3. Meredith May, "Diary of a Sex Slave," *San Francisco Chronicle,* October 8, 2006, 1.

4. Philip Meyer, *Precision Journalism: A Reporter's Introduction to Social Science Methods* (Bloomington: Indiana University Press, 1973), 3.

5. Ibid.

6. Jane Singer, "Truth and Transparency: Bloggers' Challenge to Professional Autonomy in Defining and Enacting Two Journalistic Norms," 16.

7. Melissa Wall, "'Blogs of War': Weblogs as News," *Journalism: Theory, Practice and Criticism* 6, no. 2 (2005), 154.

8. *Time,* December 25, 2006.

9. Singer, *Truth and Transparency,* 15.

10. David Broder, *Behind the Front Page* (New York: Simon and Schuster, 1987), 14–15.

11. Ibid.

12. Ibid.

13. Bill Kovach and Tom Rosenstiel, *The Elements of Journalism,* 80.

14. Epstein, *Between Fact and Fiction: The Problem of Journalism,* 16.

15. Ibid., 17.

16. Evan Cornog, "Let's Blame the Readers," *Columbia Journalism Review,* January/February 2005, 49.

17. Thomas Griffith, *The Waist-High Culture,* 66.

BIBLIOGRAPHY

◈

BOOKS

Bird, S. Elizabeth. *For Enquiring Minds: A Cultural Study of Supermarket Tabloids.* Knoxville: University of Tennessee Press, 1992.

Boswell, James. *The Life of Samuel Johnson.* New York: Random House, 1952.

Boylan, James. *Pulitzer's School: Columbia University's School of Journalism, 1903–2003.* New York: Columbia University Press, 2003.

Bradlee, Ben. *A Good Life.* New York: Touchstone, 1995.

Broder, David. *Behind the Front Page.* New York: Simon and Schuster, 1987.

Burke, Thomas F. *Lawyers, Lawsuits and Legal Rights: The Battle over Litigation in American Society.* Berkeley: University of California Press, 2002.

Calder, Iain. *The Untold Story: My 20 Years Running the National Enquirer.* New York: Hyperion, 2004.

Cerf, Christopher, and Victor Navasky. *The Experts Speak: The Definitive Compendium of Authoritative Misinformation.* New York: Villard, 1998.

Chambers, Robert. *The Book of Days* (1969), http://www.thebookof days.com.

Collingwood, R. G. *The Idea of History,* rev. ed. Oxford: Oxford University Press, 1994.

Epstein, Edward J. *Between Fact and Fiction: The Problem of Journalism.* New York: Vintage Books, 1975.

Fuller, Jack. *News Values.* Chicago: University of Chicago Press, 1996.

Garment, Suzanne. *Scandal: The Culture of Mistrust in American Politics.* New York: New York Times Books, 1991.

Gilderhus, Mark T. *History and Historians,* 5th ed. Upper Saddle River, N.J.: Prentice Hall, 2003.

Goldstein, Tom. *The News at Any Cost.* New York: Simon and Schuster, 1985.

Gore, Al. *An Inconvenient Truth.* Emmaus, Pa.: Rodale, 2006.

Graham, Katherine. *Personal History.* New York: Alfred A. Knopf, 1997.

Griffith, Thomas. *The Waist-High Culture.* New York: Harper and Brothers, 1959.

Haltom, William, and Michael McCann. *Distorting the Law.* Chicago: University of Chicago Press, 2004.

Henry, Neil. *American Carnival: Journalism Under Siege in an Age of New Media.* Berkeley: University of California Press, 2007.

Hoselitz, Bert, ed. *A Reader's Guide to the Social Sciences.* New York: Free Press, 1959.

Howard, Philip K. *The Death of Common Sense.* New York: Random House, 1995.

Hutchins, Robert Maynard. *A Free and Responsible Press.* 1947. Midway Reprint Series, Robert D. Leigh, ed. Chicago: University of Chicago Press, 1974.

Idler, no. 30 (November 11, 1758).

Kerrane, Kevin, and Yagoda, Ben, eds. *The Art of the Fact.* New York: Scribner, 1997.

Knightley, Phillip. *The First Casualty: The War Correspondent as Hero and Myth-Maker from the Crimea to Iraq,* 3d ed. Baltimore: Johns Hopkins University Press, 2004.

Kovach, Bill, and Tom Rosenstiel. *The Elements of Journalism.* New York: Crown, 2001.

Lasch, Christopher. *The Revolt of the Elites and the Betrayal of Democracy.* New York: W. W. Norton, 1995.

Leamer, Laurence. *King of the Night: The Life of Johnny Carson.* New York: William Morrow, 1989.

Liebling, A. J. *The Press,* 2d ed. New York: Pantheon Books, 1975.

Lippmann, Walter. *Liberty and the News.* New York: Harcourt, Brace and Howe, 1920.

———. *Public Opinion.* New York: Free Press, 1997.

Loftus, Elizabeth, and Katherine Ketcham. *Witness for the Defense.* New York: St. Martin's Press, 1991.

Malcolm, Janet. *Psychoanalysis: The Impossible Profession.* New York: Alfred A. Knopf, 1981.

————. *In the Freud Archives.* New York: Alfred A. Knopf, 1984.

————. *The Journalist and the Murderer.* New York: Alfred A. Knopf, 1990.

————. *The Silent Woman.* New York: Alfred A. Knopf, 1994.

————. *The Crime of Sheila McGough.* New York: Vintage Books, 1999.

Matthews, T. S. *The Sugar Pill.* New York: Simon and Schuster, 1959.

McEwan, Jenny. *Evidence and the Adversarial Process.* Oxford: Blackwell, 1992.

McGinniss, Joe. *Fatal Vision.* New York: New American Library, 1989.

Meyer, Philip. *Precision Journalism.* Bloomington: Indiana University Press, 1973.

Mitchell, Joseph. *Old Mr. Flood.* San Francisco: MacAdam Cage, 2005.

National News Council. *After "Jimmy's World": Tightening Up in Editing.* New York: National News Council, 1982.

————. "Who Said That?" A Report to the National News Council on the Use of Unidentified Sources. New York: National News Council, 1983.

Nevins, Allan. *The Gateway to History.* Chicago: Quadrangle Books, 1963.

Oreskes, Naomi. "The Scientific Consensus on Climate Change: How Do We Know We're Not Wrong?" in Joseph DiMento and Pamela Doughman, *Climate Change: What It Means for Us, Our Children and Our Grandchildren.* Cambridge: MIT Press, 2007.

Overholser, Geneva, and Kathleen Hall Jamieson, eds. *The Press.* Oxford: Oxford University Press, 2005.

Paulos, John Allen. *A Mathematician Reads the Newspaper.* New York: Basic Books, 1995.

Royal Commission on the Press, 1947–1949. London: His Majesty's Stationery Office, 1949.

Scanlan, Christopher. *Reporting and Writing: Basics for the 21st Century.* Orlando, Fla.: Harcourt College Publishers, 2000.

Shakespeare, William. *Hamlet.* John Dover Wilson, ed. Cambridge: Cambridge University Press, 1971.

Sheraton, Mimi. *Eating My Words: An Appetite for Life.* New York: Harper Perennial, 2004.

Smolla, Rodney. *Suing the Press.* Oxford: Oxford University Press, 1986.

Starr, Paul. *The Creation of the Media.* New York: Basic Books, 2004.

Strong, John, ed. *McCormick on Evidence,* 5th ed. St. Paul, Minn.: West, 1999.

Taylor, Paul. *See How They Run: Electing the President in an Age of Mediacracy.* New York: Alfred A. Knopf, 1990.

Tetlock, Philip. *Expert Political Judgment.* Princeton, N.J.: Princeton University Press, 2005.

Van Langenhove, Fernand. *The Growth of a Legend.* New York: G. P. Putnam's, 1916.

Winks, Robin, ed. *The Historian as Detective: Essays on Evidence.* New York: Harper and Row, 1970.

———. *The Oxford History of the British Empire,* vol. 5. Oxford: Oxford University Press, 1999.

OTHER REFERENCES

Amidon, Jim. "30 Minutes with David Kendall," *Wabash Magazine,* Fall/Winter 2001.

Arbib, Robert S., Jr. "Foreword: Christmas Bird Count," *American Birds* 26, no. 2 (April 1972), 135–136.

Asimow, Michael. "Popular Culture and the American Adversarial Ideology." Paper prepared for symposium, "How Popular Culture Teaches Americans about the Civil Justice System," Loyola School of Law, September 29, 2006.

Beard, Charles. "Written History as an Act of Faith," *American Historical Review* 39, no. 2 (January 1934), 219–231.

Bendiner, Robert. "The Law and Potter Stewart: An Interview with Justice Potter Stewart," *American Heritage,* December 1983.

Bennet, James. "Washington Nervously Awaits New Deliveries of Dirty Laundry," *New York Times,* September 6, 1998, "Week in Review," 5.

Blow, Richard, and Ari Posner. "Adventures in Fact Checking: Are You Completely Bald?" *New Republic,* September 26, 1988.

Boykoff, Maxwell, and Jules Boykoff. "Balance as Bias: Global Warming and the US Prestige Press," *Global Environmental Change* 14 (2004), 125–136.

Broder, David. "The Summer of My Discontent," *Washington Post,* August 28, 1994.

Buchanan, Edna. *New York Times,* May 25, 1991.

Canham, Erwin. "Newspapers and the News," *Commentary,* April 1959, 366–367.

Carr, David. "A Writer Is Back in the Saddle after His Fall from Grace," *New York Times,* July 28, 2004.

Cohen, Adam. "Can Oprah Change the Phony-Memoir Culture?" *New York Times,* February 14, 2006.

Cole, Jonathan. "Academic Freedom under Fire," *Daedalus,* Spring 2005.

Cooke, Janet. "Jimmy's World," *Washington Post,* September 28, 1980.

Cornog, Evan. "Let's Blame the Readers," *Columbia Journalism Review,* January/February 2005, 43–49.

Danner, Mark. "Iraq: The Real Election," *New York Review of Books,* April 28, 2005.

Davis v. Costa-Gavras et al., 654 F. Supp. 653 (S.D.N.Y. 1987).

Devlin, John. "Pesticide Spokesmen Accused of 'Lying' on Higher Bird Count," *New York Times,* August 14, 1972, 33.

Dionne, E. J. "Gary Hart: The Elusive Front-Runner," *New York Times Magazine,* May 3, 1987.

Donnellan, Jonathan, and Justin Peacock. "Truth and Consequences: First Amendment Protection for Accurate Reporting on Government Investigations," *New York Law School Law Review* 50 (2005–2006), 237–268.

Dworkin, Jeffrey. *NPR Ombudsman: "Truth with Edge?"* NPR, June 13, 2006.

Edwards v. National Audubon Society, 556 F.2nd 113 (2nd Cir.).

Elliot, Deni. "Journalistic Truth: An Essay Review," *Journal of Mass Media Ethics* 9, no. 3 (1994), 184–186.

Epstein, Richard. "Privacy, Publication, and the First Amendment: The Dangers of First Amendment Exceptionalism," *Stanford Law Review* 52 (2000), 1003.

Fassihi, Farnaz. "WSJ Reporter Fassihi's E-mail to Friends," *Poynteronline,* September 29, 2004.

Fisher, Ian. "Reporting and Surviving Iraq's Dangers," *New York Times,* July 18, 2004, Section 4, 1.

———. "Attack in Iraq: Many Versions, Obscure Truth," *New York Times,* April 26, 2004.

Frankel, Max. "Word and Image: What's New," *New York Times Magazine,* June 18, 1995.

Friedrich, Otto. "There Are oo Trees in Russia: The Function of Facts in Newsmagazines," *Harper's Magazine,* October 1964.

Gersh, Debra. "Good Journalism or Snooping," *Editor and Publisher,* May 16, 1987, 9.

Getler, Michael. "Is Balancing an Act?" *Washington Post,* October 17, 2004, B6.

Gibbs, Nancy. "Who Owns the Truth?" *Time,* September 27, 2004, 24–34.

Gillers, Stephen. "On Knowing the Basic Rules of Advocacy," *New York Times,* February 8, 2004, "Week in Review," 2.

Glaberson, William. "*Times* Criticized for Use of Tabloid Account," *New York Times,* December 23, 1994, A11.

Glasser, Ted. "Objectivity Precludes Responsibility," *Quill,* February 1984, 13–16.

Goldstein, Tom. "The Press and the Political Candidate," *Miami Herald,* May 10, 1987, C1.

———. "Going Respectable," *New York Newsday,* June 24, 1987, Part II, 3.

———. "Gore Flap the Latest in a Series of Clashes between Academic and Press Freedom," *American Editor,* April 2001.

———. "Lies, Damn Lies and Jayson Blair's Lies," *San Francisco Chronicle,* May 25, 2003, Insight, 1.

Gordon, Michael, and Judith Miller. "Threats and Responses: The Iraqis; U.S. Says Hussein Intensifies Quest for A-Bomb Parts," *New York Times,* September 8, 2002, 1.

Gottlieb, Martin. "Dangerous Liaisons: Journalists and Their Sources," *Columbia Journalism Review,* July/August 1989, 21–35.

Hersey, John. "The Legend on the License," *Yale Review,* Autumn 1980, 1–25.

Huber, Michael. "*Edwards v. Audubon Society* Twenty-Five Years Later: Whatever Happened to Neutral Reportage?" *Communications Lawyer,* Spring 2002, 15–17.

Judge, Frank. "*Fatal Vision:* Truth and Betrayal," *American Lawyer,* November 1987, 77–84.

Kerr, Peter. "John Devlin Dies; Retired Reporter," *New York Times,* August 7, 1984, D24.

Khawar v. Globe International, 57 Cal. Rptr. 2nd 277.

Kimball, Penn. "Journalism: Art, Craft, or Profession?" in K. S. Lynn, ed., *The Professions in America.* Boston: Beacon, 1963, 242–260.

Kirkpatrick, David. "Why Books Are the Hot Medium," *New York Times,* April 25, 2004.

Kornstein, Daniel. "Twisted Vision: Janet Malcolm's Upside Down View of the *Fatal Vision* Case," *Cardozo Studies in Law and Literature* 1, no. 2 (Autumn 1989), 127–156.

Lacayo, Richard. "Anecdotes Not Antidotes: Philip K. Howard Is Everyone's Favorite Anti-Regulatory Guru, but His Best-Selling Book Is Flawed," *Time,* April 10, 1995.

Lamb, David. "Into the Realm of Tabloids; Never Before Has Tabloid Journalism Been Such a Growth Industry," *Los Angeles Times,* February 13, 1992, 1.

Lang, Thomas. "Still Ambivalent after All These Years," *CJR Campaign Desk,* November 10, 2004.

Lightfoot, Linda. "Editors Hear the Roar of the Food Lion Case," *American Editor,* January-February 1997.

Lippmann, Walter, and Charles Merz. "A Test of the News," *New Republic,* August 4, 1920, 1–43.

MacDougall, Kent. "Letter to Editor: Where Does a Writer's 'Truth' Lie?" *Wall Street Journal,* July 2, 1984.

Malcolm, Janet. "Easy Time: A Glimpse at the Life of Jeffrey MacDonald, Who Is Serving Time in a Model Federal Prison," *New Yorker,* October 16, 1995, 98–108.

Marder, Nancy. "The Medical Malpractice Debate: The Jury as Scapegoat," *Loyola of Los Angeles Law Review* 38 (2004–2005), 1267–1296.

Margolick, David. "Psychoanalyst Loses Libel Suit against New Yorker," *New York Times,* November 3, 1994, 1.

Martin, Douglas. "James W. Carey, Teacher of Journalists, Dies at 71," *New York Times,* May 26, 2006, C11.

Masson v. The New Yorker Magazine, Alfred A. Knopf, Janet Malcolm, 960 F.2nd 896.

Mathews, Jay. "Just Checking," *New Republic,* May 18, 1992.

May, Meredith. "Diary of a Sex Slave," *San Francisco Chronicle,* October 8, 2006, 1.

McDowell, Edwin. "Issue and Debate: The Standards of Evidence in Book Publishing," *New York Times,* June 19, 1984.

McGee, Jim, and Tom Fiedler. "Miami Woman Is Linked to Hart," *Miami Herald,* May 3, 1987, 1.

Menand, Louis. "Everybody's an Expert," *New Yorker,* December 12, 2005.

Mencken, H. L. "Newspaper Morals," *Atlantic Monthly,* March 1914, 288–297.

———. "A Neglected Anniversary," *New York Evening Mail,* December 28, 1917, 9.

Metcalf, Slade. "He Said, She Said: 'Get It on Tape or Go to Trial' Is the Message from a Recent Supreme Court Decision on Reformatting Quotes," *Folio,* September 1, 1991.

Miranda v. Arizona, 384 U.S. 436 (1966).

Montopoli, Brian. "Falling over Backward Seeking Balance," *CJR Campaign Desk,* October 14, 2004.

Mooney, Chris. "Blinded by Science: How 'Balanced' Coverage Lets the Fringe Hijack Reality," *Columbia Journalism Review,* November/December 2004, 26.

Mydans, Seth. "Coup May Allow Thais to Take New Tack on Insurgency," *New York Times,* September 24, 2006.

New Yorker. "Check the Facts: Fact-Checking at *The New Yorker,*" 1988.

Nightline. ABC Transcript, September 3, 2004.

Nockleby, John, and Shannon Curreri. "100 Years of Conflict: The Past and Future of Tort Retrenchment." *Loyola of Los Angeles Law Review* 38 (2004–2005), 1021–1092.

Okrent, Daniel. "What Do You Know, and How Do You Know It?" *New York Times,* February 29, 2004.

Oreskes, Naomi. "The Scientific Consensus on Climate Change," *Science* 306, December 3, 2004, 1686.

Pattenden, Rosemary. "Conceptual versus Pragmatic Approaches to Hearsay," *Modern Law Review* 56, no. 2 (March 1993), 138–156.

People v. Defore, 150 N.E. 585, 587 (N.Y. 1926).

Posner, Richard. "In the Fraud Archives: The Crime of Sheila Mc-Gough," *New Republic,* April 19, 1999, 29–34.

"Q & A: Gay Talese." *SI.com,* May 25, 2006.

Reid, Alastair. "Letter from Barcelona," *New Yorker,* December 2, 1961, 137.

Rosen, Jay. "Authorized Knower: Farnaz Fassihi's Accidental Baghdad Dispatch," *Pressthink,* October 8, 2004.

Russomanno, Joseph, and Kyu Ho Youm. "*Edwards v. National Audubon Society* and Libel Law: The 'Neutral Reportage' Doctrine 20 Years After." Paper presented at the annual meeting of the Association for Education in Journalism and Mass Communication, July 1997.

Rutenberg, James, and Edmund L. Andrews. "Evans Seen atop List to Head Treasury," *New York Times,* May 27, 2006, 1.

Rutten, Tim. "Private E-mail Is Public," *latimes.com,* October 2, 2004.

Sachs, Andrea. "Mud and the Mainstream," *Columbia Journalism Review,* May/June 1995.

Schudson, Michael. "Runaway Jury Awards . . . and Other Made-for-Media Myths," *Columbia Journalism Review,* July/August 2005.

Seelye, Katharine. "Agendas Clash in Bid to Alter Law on Product Liability," *nytmes.com,* September 24, 2006.

Seligman, Craig. "Janet Malcolm: In Her Relentless Pursuit of the Truth She's Left a Few Bodies in Her Wake, but Isn't That Part of a Journalist's Job?" Salon.com, February 29, 2000.

Shafer, Jack. "I Believe the *National Enquirer,* Why Don't You?" *Slate,* June 11, 2004, www.slate.com/id/2102303.

Shapiro, Susan. "This Paper Has Not Been Fact-Checked! A Study of Fact-Checking in American Magazines," Gannett Center for Media Studies, 1989.

Sheppard, Judith. "Playing Defense," *American Journalism Review,* September 1998.

Sigal, Leon. "Sources Make the News." In Robert Karl Manoff and Michael Schudson, eds., *Reading the News.* New York: Pantheon, 1987.

Siklos, Richard. "I Cannot Tell a Lie (From an Amplification)," *New York Times,* February 5, 2006, Section 3, 3.

Singer, Jane. "Truth and Transparency: Bloggers' Challenge to Professional Autonomy in Defining and Enacting Two Journalistic Norms." Paper presented at the annual meeting of the Association for Education in Journalism and Mass Communication, August 2006.

Singer, Matt. "Tales from the Hood: Boredom Abounds in Fairy-Tale Pastiche," *Village Voice,* January 10, 2006.

Smith, Dinitia. "Love Is Strange: The Crusading Feminist and the Repentant Womanizer," *New York,* March 22, 1993, 36–41.

Soloski John. "News Reporting and Professionalism: Some Constraints on the Reporting of the News," *Media, Culture and Society* 11 (1989).

Steele, Bob. *RTNDA Communicator,* April 1997.

Stephens, Mitchell. "We're All Postmodern Now," *Columbia Journalism Review,* July/August 2005, 60–64.

Stewart, James. "Consider the Sources," *New York Times Book Review,* July 4, 1999.

Stewart, James, and Laurie Michelson. "Reining in the Neutral Reportage Privilege," *Forum on Communications Law,* Summer 1999.

Stone, Geoffrey. "Above the Law: Research Methods, Ethics, and the Law of Privilege," *Sociological Methodology* 32 (2002), 19–27.

Tierney, John. "Cash on Delivery," *New York Times Magazine,* April 14, 1993, 64.

Time, Inc. v. Hill, 385 U.S. 374 (1967), 389.

Trelford, Donald. Speech (on file), March 29, 1983.

Van Natta, Don, Jr., Adam Liptak, and Clifford J. Levy. "The Miller Case: A Notebook, a Cause, a Jail Cell and a Deal," *New York Times,* October 16, 2005, 1.

Wall, Melissa. "'Blogs of War': Weblogs as News." *Journalism: Theory, Practice and Criticism* 6, no. 2 (2005), 153–172.

Weinberg, Steve. "Why Books Err So Often," *Columbia Journalism Review,* July/April 1998.

Weinstein, Jack. Order and Judgment, *United States v. Louis Eppolito and Stephen Caracappa,* June 30, 2006.

Wells, Gary, and Elizabeth Olson. "Eyewitness Testimony," *Annual Review of Psychology* (2003), 277–295.

Wines, Michael. "To Fill Notebooks, and Then a Few Bellies," *New York Times,* August 27, 2006, "Week in Review," 1.

INDEX

◈

Tom Goldstein is a professor of journalism and mass communications and director of the Mass Communications Program at the University of California at Berkeley. He is the former dean of both the Graduate School of Journalism at Columbia University and the Graduate School of Journalism at the University of California at Berkeley, the author of *A Two-Faced Press?* and *The News at Any Cost,* the coauthor of *The Lawyers' Guide to Writing Well,* and the editor of *Killing the Messenger: 100 Years of Media Criticism.*

Howard H. Baker, Jr., is a former U.S. senator, presidential chief of staff, and U.S. ambassador. The former vice chairman of the Senate Watergate Committee, he is the author of *No Margin for Error: America in the Eighties, Howard Baker's Washington: An Intimate Portrait of the Nation's Capital City,* and *Scott's Gulf.*